Bodies in the Making

Transgressions
and
Transformations

———○———

Nancy N. Chen
and
Helene Moglen

editors

new pacific press
Santa Cruz, California
2006

Published and distributed in the United States by
New Pacific Press
204 Locust Street
Santa Cruz, CA 95060

www.literaryguillotine.com/npp/npphome.html

First published 2006

10 9 8 7 6 5 4 3 2 1

New Pacific Press was established in 2003 as a "Hey, we'll at
least break even" alternative to the commercial, homogeneous
publications that currently dominate the publishing industry.
New Pacific Press does not believe that it necessarily serves
the public interest to operate a not-for-profit enterprise, but
rather that there is both value and viability in publishing
small, innovative, educational and culturally significant
works that the mainstream may consider small potatoes.
Our planned publications will be primarily sociopolitical,
economic, cultural studies; they will be scholarly, personal,
poetic, mixed-media presentations that reflect the multiplicity
of cultural work being done in the greater Bay Area and
throughout the Pacific Rim(s).

Cover photograph by James Day

Book design by Stephen Pollard
Set in Hiroshige and Reliq

ISBN 0-9712546-3-x

Printed in Canada by Hignell Book Printing

Contents

Acknowledgements

Bodies in the Making: Transgressions and Transformations began with a conference, which in turn began with a planning group, both sponsored by the Institute for Advanced Feminist Research (IAFR) at the University of California Santa Cruz. Joyce Brodsky, Nancy Chen, Maria Frangos, John Marlovits, Helene Moglen, Sheila Namir, Katharine Norwood, and Mary Weaver met, read, talked and strategized for almost a year—and then enjoyed the double flowering that their collective energies produced. Elizabeth Alsberg anchored the efforts that shaped the conference and the book, and Katharine Norwood, the Assistant Director of the institute, facilitated every aspect of the project with her creative interventions and good humor.

The book's co-editors are particularly grateful to Jody Greene, who edits the IAFR series, Feminist Provocations, in which *Bodies in the Making* appears, and to Erin Murphy, who designed the provocative conference poster and book cover. We also thank the numerous UCSC units that joined the IAFR and the University of California Humanities Research Institute at Irvine with their conference support.

For the publication of *Bodies in the Making,* the co-editors are indebted to David Watson, proprietor of The Literary Guillotine bookstore and founder of the innovative New Pacific Press, both of which occupy a central place in the intellectual and expressive life of a community they have helped to create. Thanks also to Stephen Pollard for his design and production work. To collaborate with David and Stephen is to rediscover the pleasures of book making, which writers and editors have largely lost.

Introduction

Bodies—Inside and Out

Helene Moglen and *Nancy Chen*

This volume offers fresh perspectives on body modifications that are neither voluntary nor involuntary—but somewhere in between. Over the last two decades, social theorists and scholars of medicine have focused on bodies as sites of power and self-making. They have concentrated on issues of agency and subjectivity raised by the proliferation of such practices as tattooing, piercing, anorexia, self-cutting, plastic surgery, scarification, body-building, prosthetics, organ transplants and life extension technologies. Most recently, the increased availability and mainstreaming of modification technologies in the popular media, across ethnic groups and beyond the U.S. have mandated a global view of the expanding beauty and plastic surgery industries and the international dissemination of biomedicine. In reframing debates about body modification beyond the binaries of mind-body and elective or coerced, contributors to this collection offer new approaches to bodily transformation across normative categories of age, race, national identity, gender and sexuality.

Instead of presuming that body practices have uniform meanings, contributors emphasize the importance of psycho-social influences in shaping body projects that rely on techno-logical, medical and artistic invention. Insisting on the relation of phenomena that are often treated as distinct—cosmetic surgery and tattooing, for example, or aging, illness, pharmaceutical intervention, and warfare—the authors show, from intergenerational and intersubjective perspectives, how body modification technologies cut across differences, while they also undermine or even fetishize them.

As the authors examine a range of physical transformations, they tend to frame them not as individualized practices or transgressions but as reflections of specific political and cultural moments. They ask how appropriate it is to use languages of normalcy and pathology to describe particular forms of modification and, if it is appropriate, when. They ask whether various transformational practices signal increased sovereignty over lives, or if self-determination is an illusion that disguises more invidious forms of social control. They explore how media promotion of "makeovers" and reality programs, which are aimed at the achievement of desirable bodies, may coincide with deepening forms of medicalization that promote violence in the name of beauty. They observe that the need to belong and the perils of nonconformity encourage the imposition of heightened standards of perfection, which support consumption fueled by inequality. While some essays in this volume address ways in which body modifications may be involuntary—in aging, for example, and in illness or warfare—others clearly indicate the extent to which recent forms of medical intervention—such as organ transplantation, anti-aging techniques, or prosthetic technology—blur the boundaries between elective and involuntary modifications and underscore questions of who deserves or can afford a normative body.

In sum, these essays reject Cartesian dualism, representing bodies that are constructed within institutional spaces through individual practices of embodiment. Contributors identify alternative ways of theorizing the relationship of bodies, culture and subjectivity in order to engage critically with innovative and longstanding forms of bodily revision. Ultimately, the volume reenacts the culture's obsession with bodies while it reveals the power dynamics that drive the beliefs and practices of their diverse but related transformations.

The five sections of *Bodies in the Making: Transgressions and Transformations* largely reproduce the conference sessions for which the essays were prepared. Although some concepts and problems defy strict categorization and persistently reappear, the varying perspectives of the authors are equally persistent in converting familiar ideas into fresh theoretical possibilities.

The essays in the book's first section, "The Rhetoric of the Pose: Rethinking Hannah Wilke," present personal and theoretical responses to a posthumous exhibition of photographs, videos, and mixed media by and about Hannah Wilke, which was curated by Shelby Graham and Joyce Brodsky. Shelby Graham introduces essays by Joyce Brodsky, Carla Freccero and Joanna Frueh, all of whom consider what it meant to Wilke—and what it means to contemporary viewers— that the artist used her body as the medium and the meaning of a lifelong autobiographical narrative that ended with her physical debility and death.

The second section of the collection, "Skin: Cosmetic Surgery and Tattooing," focuses on modifications of the skin's surface and asks what these modifications tell us about the interrelation of self-presentation, ideology and psychology. Victoria Pitts establishes the parameters of the discussion in "Beauty, Body Image and Psychosocial Power." Here she examines the power relations that construct subjects of cosmetic surgery, and she explores the social functions that increasing medicalization and pathologizing have performed. Turning the implications of cosmetic surgery inside out, Pitts shows how psychological meanings are inscribed on bodies that cultural and economic values of the beauty industry have produced. In "Love My Neighbor, Hate Myself: The Vicissitudes of Affect in Cosmetic Surgery," Virginia Blum argues that it is largely through the normalizing influence of television that cosmetic surgery is no longer understood as an expression of vanity. Instead, it has become a route to self-improvement, well-being and happiness, with self-loathing converted to self-love along the way. Employing a Lacanian view of self-formation,

Blum asserts that cosmetic surgery makes it possible for the client to transform the alien aspect of her self *into* an ideal other. Maria Frangos is also interested in the psychological and social implications of cosmetic surgery in the context of reality makeover shows. In "Embodied Subjectivity and the Quest for Self in Televised Narratives of Body Modification," she extends the topic by comparing programs that focus on surgical body modification with those that treat sex and species transformation. She examines the radically different ways in which women who undergo cosmetic surgery and men and women who undergo transsexual surgery think about their own subjectivities in relation to their interior and physical selves. In an interview with Mary Weaver, the writer and actress Aleshia Brevard writes from a participant's perspective. She reflects on differences between her feelings about her own gender reassignment surgery, which she sees as "life-saving," and "the nips and tucks" she has had throughout her life in order to accommodate to a culture that values youth and beauty. She also considers the limited meaning that transsexuality had for her in the past, and she compares it to more expansive definitions and practices for which transsexuals are advocating in the present. Finally, Kelley Richardson writes about "The Santa Cruz Tattoo Project," for which she has photographed and interviewed hundreds of people. In her essay she explains how a phrase glimpsed on a license plate frame—"We are not our bodies"—speaks to a belief that motivates many who choose tattooing as a transformative expression of themselves. This phrase is given meaning in Richardson's own essay as it is in her images, which provide a sense of the libratory power of this particular form of expressive culture.

The five essays in the section "Inside/Outside" explore the usefulness and inadequacies of an oppositional metaphor in engaging the body/mind relation and issues of subjectivity and embodiment. Three of the essays consider the function of self-cutting in diverse populations and contexts. In "Embodiments and Disembodiments: The Relation of Body Modifications to Two Psychoanalytic Treatments," Sheila Namir describes the experience of the "bodymind" in psychoanalytic therapy from the perspectives of an analyst and a patient. Insisting that psychological work is intersubjectively determined and involves the body as well as the mind and its affects, she explores successful and unsuccessful therapeutic experiences of embodiment. Discussing self-cutting, tattooing and cosmetic surgery in this context, she shows how body modifications can have important implications for the development and progress of the therapeutic relationship. In "Cutting Through Race and Class: Women of Color and Self-Injury," Gabriela Sandoval counters the popular view that self-cutting is a problem that only affects educated, middle class, white women. She examines this practice—which she designates as self-injurious behavior—in less privileged Latina students who are the first in their families to attend university. Theorizing about the cultural function that self-cutting serves in these young women's lives, she emphasizes the importance of studying behaviors of this sort in their specific racial, sexual and socioeconomic contexts. In "Borderlines In and Of the Prison," Lorna Rhodes focuses on a prison Mental Health Unit in which men, who are usually diagnosed as "borderlines," cut, mutilate and otherwise harm themselves, creating medical emergencies that produce a chain of predictable bureaucratic responses. She examines the particular functions that self-cutting serves in this alienated physical environment and she shows how that environment is mirrored in the psychic structures of prisoners as well as in responses to them and their behaviors on the part of staff.

The last two papers in this section engage the inside-outside dilemma from different perspectives: the first considering the effects of psychopharmaceuticals on the body and the second analyzing alien identity in popular culture. In

"'Recovery for What?' On Drugs and Psychopharmafetishism," John Marlovits shows how the use of psychopharmaceuticals in a clinical environment constructs a passive subject whose search for mental health is characterized by perpetual waiting and deferred expectations. He also explains how the staff's efforts to combat the use of illicit drugs and drug addiction rests on the containment and disavowal of the social and political histories of specific drugs and on the advancement of an implicitly normative model of white minds and bodies. Finally, in "The Other Inside," Carla Freccero sets out to deconstruct the conventional mind/body, inside/outside opposition in order to analyze "the other inside," which is a form of identificatory embodiment. Using the science-fiction film series Alien as her focus, she examines the meaning of embodied subjectivity in terms of alien inhabitation and she asks what it tells us about the nature of the human and the politics of relationality.

The essays in the fourth section, "Social Bodies and Transformation," consider the moral and psychological implications of legacies of the body, trying—in two cases—to imagine ways of re-conceptualizing conventional structures of relationship and processes of subjectification. In "Aged Bodies and Kinship Matters: The Biologization of Moral Commitment," Sharon Kaufman examines—with her two co-authors—the moral and social dilemmas that have emerged as a consequence of the normalization of kidney transplantation as a clinical and cultural practice. Studying the implications of choice from the perspective of donors and recipients, they also consider the relation of class to changing expectations of the right to longer lives. In "Aging and Trans-aging," Helene Moglen also invokes the self/other relation as she reflects on ways in which one becomes, as one ages, both strange and familiar to oneself. Rejecting a melancholic relation to aging, she urges the adoption of a model of trans-aging that emphasizes the constant, erratic movement that takes place in consciousness across, between and among the endlessly overlapping stages of life. In "A Note of a Sportswriter's Daughter: Companion

Species" Donna Haraway writes about bodies that are made through inheritance in the flesh and through the linking of "looping ontics and antics" that shape the collaborative relations of companion species. Drawing out her comparison between the bodymind connections of companion species and kin, she shows how crucial the "regard" of one for the other is to the solidity and depth of both forms of relationship.

The essays in the collection's last section, "Bodies and Violence," focus on painful modifications of the body/mind that are inflicted by the violence of war and other forms of culture. In "Hillbilly Armour and C-Legs: Technologies and Bodies at War," Steve Kurzman argues that important advances in prosthetics technology and rehabilitative care for amputees has not primarily been driven by the number of casualties that the war in Iraq has produced. Instead, the prime motivator is the protracted guerrilla war, with the interaction of Humvees, improvised explosive devices, and body armor, which have changed the way in which bodies are wounded. Although public attention has been focused on the quality of technology used in combat, Kurzman is concerned with the long-term costs and consequences of such advanced technologies for actual bodies. In "Nursing Memory: Who Deserves to Heal and After Which War(s)?" Megan Moodie explains how narratives of women veterans have changed from the genre of heterosexual romance to one of trauma and recovery. Focusing on women who have spoken publicly of the sexual trauma they endured in the military, she considers the bureaucratic response to such narratives, which includes the denial of benefits that would facilitate healing. In this situation, Moodie perceives a familiar form of social will that intends to make the suffering of the vulnerable invisible. Finally, in "Dead Bodies, Violence, and Living On through Plastination," Nancy Chen reflects on the increasing interest in dead bodies in the US and other cultures, and the information about the human they provide, Concerned with stories about dead bodies that are told through new technologies of viewing, she focuses on the process of plastination, In this context, she looks at the range of cultural attitudes that promote the production, circulation and consumption of preserved corpses, which deconstruct the boundary between life and death.

In sum, then, *Bodies in the Making* complements existing work by examining the relation of material and representational practices that are commonly seen as disparate and unlike. Employing a range of interpretive strategies (psychoanalytic and social theory, medical discourse and praxis, popular culture and the politics of everyday life), the authors refuse familiar oppositions between body and mind, the psychological and the social, pathology and normalcy, and voluntary and involuntary behavior. Taken together, the essays expose some of the limits and possibilities of body modification at the same time that they provide new ways of understanding embodiment and being in the world.

I

The Rhetoric of the Pose:
Rethinking Hannah Wilke

1

Introducing
The Rhetoric of the Pose[1]

Shelby Graham

Hannah Wilke used her body as narrative. She made us pay attention to the rhetoric of her gestures in the 1970s and 1980s and she held our attention during her struggle with cancer in the 1990s. Wilke was a cross-media practitioner: she worked confidently in all media from sculpture to video performance. She combined wit, politics, art history, eroticism, beauty, kitsch and autobiography. *The Rhetoric of the Pose: Rethinking Hannah Wilke*, a posthumous exhibition of Wilke's work spanning 1974 to 1992, includes photographs, mixed media, and videos of Wilke's performance art as well as large color prints of her mother and of Wilke herself in the stages of physical decline and death from cancer. Hannah Wilke's work is as vital today as in the past; it has been an honor to exhibit it at the University of California Santa Cruz. I would like to thank Marsie Scharlatt (Hannah Wilke's sister) and her family of the Hannah Wilke Collection and Archive in Los Angeles for loaning the works on exhibition and for granting permission to publish the following images.[2] I would also like to thank SolwayJones Gallery, Los Angeles, for providing the images.

As Hannah Wilke said, "My work has always been about language." Wilke manipulates language in the titles of

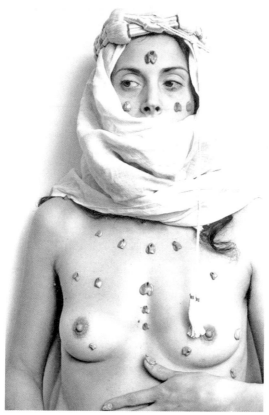

SOS Starification Object Series (Veil), 1974

works such as *SOS Starification Object Series* with its play on scarification and disfigurement; *Super-t-Art*, with its reference to *Jesus Christ SuperStar*; and her final series, *Intra-Venus*, with her fierce gaze and powerful pose haunted by the fragility of illness. The following essays, presented at the first panel of the IAFR conference by Joyce Brodsky, Carla Freccero, and Joanna Frueh, rethink the work of Hannah Wilke and re-examine the rhetoric of the pose. The authors describe the complexity of Wilke's use of her own body as both subject and object and the modifications of her body both willed and as the result of disease. We are considering these issues to understand the meaning of Wilke's art for contemporary viewers. In her paper, "Painful Viewing: Hannah Wilke and Susan Sontag," Joyce Brodsky, professor emerita of the art department at UCSC, positions Hannah Wilke's *Intra-Venus* work in relation to questions raised by Susan Sontag; Carla Freccero, professor of literature at UCSC, gives Wilke the opportunity to respond defiantly to 1970s feminist critics in her essay, "De-Idealizing the Body"; and Joanna Frueh, art historian, writer, and performance artist, gives Wilke the platform to offer and attack her own beauty in her essay, "Beauty Loves Company."

Hannah Wilke's work is not about death; it is about celebrating life and allowing our bodies to tell stories.

Notes

1. *The Rhetoric of the Pose: Rethinking Hannah Wilke:* exhibition curated by Joyce Brodsky and Shelby Graham, October 5–December 3, 2005, Mary Porter Sesnon Art Gallery, University of California Santa Cruz. Panel discussion, October 14, 2005.

2. Credits for Hannah Wilke:

Page 3: *SOS Starification Object Series (Veil)*, 1974; gelatin silver print; 40 × 27 inches. Copyright © Marsie, Emanuelle, Damon and Andrew Scharlatt; licensed by VAGA, New York, NY. Hannah Wilke Collection and Archive, Los Angeles; courtesy SolwayJones.

Page 7: *Intra-Venus #6*, February 19, 1992; chromagenic supergloss print with overlaminate; 47½ × 71½ inches, edition 1/3. Hannah Wilke Collection and Archive, Los Angeles; courtesy SolwayJones. Copyright © Donald Goddard.

Page 16: *Intra-Venus #4*, July 26, 1992–February 19, 1992; chromagenic supergloss prints with overlaminate; two panels, 71½ × 47½ inches each, edition 1/3. Hannah Wilke Collection and Archive, Los Angeles; courtesy SolwayJones. Copyright © Donald Goddard.

Page 21: *Super-t-Art*, 1974; twenty black-and-white photographs, AP; 6½ × 4½ inches each, 40½ × 32½ inches overall. Copyright © Marsie, Emanuelle, Damon and Andrew Scharlatt; licensed by VAGA, New York, NY. Hannah Wilke Collection and Archive, Los Angeles; courtesy SolwayJones.

2

Painful Viewing: Hannah Wilke and Susan Sontag

Joyce Brodsky

When I first encountered the photographs taken of Hannah Wilke's cancer-ridden body in the performalist self-portrait series she called *Intra-Venus*, I had a visceral reaction so potent—tears and nausea—that I quickly turned away from them.[1] Subsequent viewings, while still experientially intense, enabled me to ask the following questions: Is my "painful viewing" of atrocities perpetrated on the body—both natural and afflicted—only an anaesthetizing surrogate for the moral responsibility of acting instead of merely looking and feeling awful? In particular, does Susan Sontag's indictment of traumatic photography, which only "corroborates what it records," apply as well to the painful viewing that makes me believe that I know something about the "real" sufferings of the pictured other?[2] In addition, how has my bodily perception been modified by the constant reception of images of torture, violation and disease that are ubiquitous, and how does that shape the way in which I react to Wilke's photographs today?

In this brief essay, I will use Susan Sontag's still relevant and still brilliant critique *On Photography* (1977)—and the more recent *Regarding the Pain of Others* (2003)—to read the last works of Hannah Wilke, and aspects of her other photography.[3] I am interested in the way that rethinking Wilke's work centers the viewer's body through the perception of traumatic images. I also want to consider the relevance of Sontag's critique of voyeurism—which she posits as intrinsic to the photographic enterprise—to the viewer's experience of the earlier photographs of Wilke's beautiful, nude figure.

While there are profound insights about the nature of reality and important moral questions raised on every page of *On Photography*, Susan Sontag focuses on three important issues that are particularly relevant to Wilke's "performalist self-portraits." The first relates to appropriation and power. "To photograph is to appropriate the thing photographed. It means putting oneself into a certain relation to the world that feels like knowledge—and, therefore, like power" (p. 4). If photographing others is a kind of knowledge/power activity that appropriates and objectifies, what happens when the "other" that is the subject is oneself? In every work that entailed being videoed or photographed, not only was Wilke the willing subject, but she had control over all aspects of the project. It is important to note that most of Wilke's public photographs are of herself; she did not use the camera as a machine that pictured others, willing subjects or not. While it is obviously a very different form of photographing then taking pictures of the wounded and dying in natural or man-made catastrophes, Wilke's process does suggest that photography may not be *intrinsically* about the power of appropriation, although it is generally used in that manner.

Sontag's discussion of the pictures of war or upheaval that photographers take at the moment when someone is, for example, being abused or tortured or is dying are, for her, images of complicity. Instead of interceding, the photographer watches through the camera's eye for the perfect moment to snap the shutter. In *Regarding the Pain of Others*, she cites examples in the history of war photography that seem morally more horrific because she finds that many of the most famous pictures were artificially arranged even to the moving of dead bodies, or the reenactment of a battle scene to make the image more dramatic.[4] Her discussion of the viewer's encounter with and reaction to traumatic pictures has now become our commonplace response. Too many visual horrors reach us in too many media forms so that we have become inured to feelings or, even worse, we have acquired the appetite for raising the ante. If at first the "normal" reaction may be revulsion and compassion, repetition cools the fervor and we may look without having an affective response. Is that the final result of power/knowledge?

I have documented above my first reaction to Hannah Wilke's *Intra-Venus Series* photographs, and others have told me about their similar responses. However, I keep looking at them because they refuse to be cooled down; they encapsulate a different kind of power/knowledge, and they refuse the

Intra-Venus #6, February 19, 1992

sentimentality and banality that often replace repetitious viewing, even of the horrific. Wilke's iconic and indexical images portray—in part, through their confrontational scale— an amazing strength and self-awareness. It must have been this that allowed her to record herself dying of cancer through ironic comparisons to her former, beautiful body, in some of the very same poses she assumed in her early photography and videos. Their form of power/knowledge is rooted in the specifics of her situation, and in my encounter I want to penetrate their surfaces in the face of my still-felt anguish. Unlike the traumatic photography that only "corroborates what it records," which we either turn from, passively gaze at, or become voyeuristic monsters wanting more, Wilke's *Intra-Venus* portraits are visually and conceptually complex. Their scale and presence affects me through body awareness—the voyeuristic replaced by my "being there" in the flesh before them. Then I perceive what aging and disease can do to the "institutionally" formed concept of the female body that Wilke parodies in her earlier work. With rapidity, many more crucial concerns emerge.

The second quote from Sontag about aging and death reverberates back and forth in my mind as I look from the slender, youthful body to the bloated figure ravaged by disease.

> Through photographs we follow in the most intimate, troubling way the reality of how people age. To look at an old photograph of oneself, of anyone one has known, or of a much photographed public person is to feel first of all: how much younger I (she, he) was then. Photography is the inventory of mortality" (p. 70).

From photographs of her gorgeous body marked/scarred with chewing-gum cunts to the last photographs of 1991–92 shot by her husband Donald Goddard, a picture album is formed that compares youthful, aging and diseased flesh in ways unlike any other work with which I am familiar.[5] However, in contrast to Sontag's inventory of mortality usually associated with family albums or media exposures of aging celebrities (one of the most heartless is that of the not-so-aged but haggard Ava Gardner trying to hide from potential viewers on an airplane) these are anything but album pictures or the "caught unawares" that plague aging or ill celebrity. Instead, I think they are about the body that Wilke loved even as she mapped the stages of her flesh ravaged by disease.[6] How could she have performed as Venus in *Intra-Venus Series No. 1*, or presented herself as a glamour girl; or have been robed as the Madonna. How could she have looked at us almost seductively through the few strands left from her magnificent head of hair? How could she have allowed us to encounter what may be the most difficult images, those of her bloated and scarred flesh in some of the last photographs, if she denied herself love and admiration. I think she loved her own body from the very beginning, and flaunted it through the rhetoric of the pose as an instrument of female power and sexuality.[7] I admit to erotic feelings when I looked at Hannah Wilke's body in her early works (of course being straight means never admitting that one is aroused by the female body). However, it is not the eroticism of the voyeuristic that touched me, but the eroticism enabled by her audacity, self-love and, even more importantly, her nude flesh stamped with cunt emblems/scars she pasted on both as an act of revelation and of feminist outrage.

The last quote from Sontag returns me to my initial experience before Wilke's *Intra-Venus* photographs and it is inclusive of the other two.

> Photographs shock insofar as they show something novel. Unfortunately, the ante keeps getting raised—partly through the very proliferation of such images of horror. One's first encounter with the photographic inventory of ultimate horror is a kind of revelation, the prototypically modern revelation: a negative epiphany (p. 19).

Hannah Wilke's *Intra-Venus Series* photographs shock and they are novel, but they prohibit that negative epiphany because they are always emphatically present, and they escape the voyeuristic by refusing the gaze. In these and many other ways, this body of work saves photography from Sontag's often-justifiable indictment. These portrayals also escape the shift to metaphor that Sontag addresses in her essay *Illness as Metaphor*.[8] Wilke refuses that escape because she controls the rhetoric of her pose. The photograph is embodied not only because of the indexical nature of photography in the pre-digital age, but also through the power she projects to hold the viewer in the intended encounter.

As a consequence of repeated viewing, her photographs have enabled me to take stock of my aging flesh, deeply situated in my sags and wrinkles. While never beautiful like Hannah, yet like her in her last pictures, I reckon with a modified body—sometimes in admiration—that is still with me in the here and now. As to the horrific images that the media presents to me every day, I need to stop in front of some of them—not in front of all, because that would preclude psychic survival—to try to perceive in my body what it was like being there. This I have learned from facing Hannah Wilke's photographs. In *Regarding the Pain of Others* (p. 118) Sontag addresses some aspects of her own critique *On Photography*. I use her words to end this essay because they are so relevant to my experiences encountering Wilke's *Intra-Venus Series* photographs.

It is felt that there is something morally wrong with the abstract reality offered by photography: that one has no right to experience the suffering of others at a distance . . . the standing back from the aggressiveness of the world which frees us for observation and for elective attention . . . There's nothing wrong with standing back and thinking. To paraphrase several sages: "Nobody can think and hit someone at the same time."

Notes

1. Wilke entitled a photograph of herself nude at the age of four *First Performalist Self-Portrait* in her retrospective at the University of Missouri in 1989. See the catalogue for the exhibition by Thomas H. Kochheiser, ed., *Hannah Wilke: A Retrospective* (Columbia: University of Missouri Press, 1989), p. 67.

2. I am indebted to the recent article by Sharon Sliwinski, "A painful labor: responsibility and photography," *Visual Studies*, 19/2, 2004, pp. 150–161.

3. Susan Sontag, *On Photography* (New York: Farrar, Strauss and Giroux, 1977). *Regarding the Pain of Others* (New York: Farrar, Strauss and Giroux, 2003).

4. Sontag, *Regarding the Pain of Others*, p. 63 and *passim*. At the end of the book (p. 124) she gives a compelling description of one such "visionary photowork" that she believes makes even this enterprise important. This is a clue to understanding how complex was her involvement with photography.

5. High points in that album would include those in *SOS Starification Object Series*, 1974–82, with the chewing gum cunts; enacting the rhetoric of posing in Hannah Wilke: *Super-t-Art*; and videoed doing a striptease routine *Through the Large Glass* of 1974 (behind Marcel Duchamp's *The Bride Stripped Bare . . .*).

6. Her sister Marsie Scharlatt talked to me about the pain and suffering Hannah faced, and I do not mean to ignore the despair she must have felt every day of these last months.

7. See note 1.

8. Susan Sontag, *Illness as Metaphor and AIDS and Its Metaphors* (New York: Doubleday, 1990).

3

De-Idealizing the Body: Hannah Wilke, 1940–1993

Carla Freccero

This paper is about retrospective glances. I have only just begun to look at Hannah Wilke's performance art and images. I am seeing the work from an endpoint, an end point that re-reads and even re-writes this body of work, and I am trying to understand what alternative glances, understandings, appraisals might occur—might have occurred—had I not been looking backward. Retrospectivity creates a kind of narrative teleology leading, somehow, inexorably, from a beginning to an end. It is in a way ironic to perform a retrospective on a collection of images, since portrait photography is, like lyric poetry, often thought of as precisely what seeks to counter and arrest the drive to narrativize. This is not to say we can escape the look that sees from the perspective of the history that will be. But I want to ask questions about what emerges as I resist the retrospectivity of my own gaze at Hannah Wilke's work.

At the opening, I heard folks say: "Watch out, get ready, this is going to be tough," presumably because there's a temporal narrative here, a narrative about beauty's demise at the hands of an alien inhabitation we fear and respond to phobically with our eyes averted: cancer. Medusa was once a beautiful woman, you couldn't take your eyes off her; later, as a punishment for being raped, Ovid says, she became the terrifying snake-haired woman. You had to look away or you would be turned to stone. Indeed, the story goes, Perseus used her severed head as a weapon to stun his enemies in battle.

I hear that back in the seventies, when Wilke was putting various kinds of second-wave and Marxist feminist theories into practice, she was criticized in some corners for colluding with exploitative regimes of representation by displaying idealized images of her own face and body. And all through that time she was also talking back to her feminist critics, as *Beware Fascist Feminism* suggests. Nowadays pro-sex feminists, often radical sex lesbians who were active in the seventies and eighties such as Dorothy Allison and Cherrie Moraga, not to mention the other Angry Women visual and performance artists of Wilke's era (Judy Chicago, Carolee Schneeman, Adrian Piper, Ana Mendieta, and we might even mention Annie Sprinkle's apprenticeship for her future work here) have had their say and their day. They are—or would be—in a position to look back over the repressive anti-porn anti-feminist eighties and say, as Gayle Rubin once put it, "we told you so!"

The anti-porn feminist movement and the lesbian feminism of the seventies and eighties that bore with difficulty the contradictions of female/feminist representation found themselves frighteningly in bed with some of the most fascist and fundamentally Christian paternalist elements of US culture, working together to efface risky representation from the public sphere. Wilke can be thought of as part of that movement we don't hear as much about, the one where angry women feminists claimed agency and embraced sexual risk squarely within the contradictions of a phallocratic culture. It's nevertheless somewhat unusual to see the work of a feminist so exactly inhabiting and miming idealized heterosexualizing regimes of representation in these terms. And it's perhaps precisely the heterosexualization of Wilke's images of the female body and face as object that renders those images at times ambivalent with regard to the very regimes they seem to want to critique.

In *Hannah Wilke*, Joanna Frueh writes that "Wilke began performing and having herself photographed nude in 1970, after her mother's mastectomy."[1] When I learned this, something in her work became clearer to me, as a retrospective perception. Watch her poses, see the anger in that pretty body and face, see the obsessive and repeated capture of the images of body and face all through the seventies and eighties. So, for example, the *SOS Starification Object Series* could be read as a semi-playful feminist indictment on the ordinary kinds of degradations to which women are subjected through the image of the chewed-up piece of gum stuck on the body as though it were the underside of a table or a chair, the chewed-up piece of gum miming the vulva that is the object of such degradation. Note too how, although this piece has some of the essentializing and universalizing "sisterhood is global" tendencies of a certain era of US liberal feminism, it is also more progressive than some forms of liberal feminism today, for it does not assume the posture of the enlightened western woman maternalistically pitying her third-world sisters. But something more personal in the series might be seen to play powerfully and melancholically on wounding and scarification, invoking the vulnerability of the female body to disfigurement, whether through aging or through traumatic processes. In this retrospective context, then, that body is already suffused with both subjectivity and temporality, and though it may pose as "the" idealized female nude, it is haunted by a knowledge of its fragility that renders it defiant. It is a vulnerability rendered especially predictively poignant for daughters of breast cancer survivors, who sense they may literally inherit the maternal wound.

Fragility and defiance persist through Wilke's later work that documents—in its historical specificity as the image of a singular and particular being—the diseased and dying body. Such images, through their retroactive citation of the idealizing surfaces of the earlier work, continue, cite and refigure western aestheticizations of the female form. In this way, Wilke also lends beauty—the elusive and ephemeral beauty of the traditionally idealized, exemplary, female body—to a female embodiment fully saturated with history and time. For these images are themselves quite beautiful I think.

Thus, as a body of work across a span of time (some two decades), Hannah Wilke's images de-idealize the female body, restore to it historicity and temporality, in part through the pseudo-documentation of her own bodily image, especially her face, through health and disease. Whereas dominant traditions of visually representing the female body idealize the body by de-realizing it—making it timeless, smooth, seamless, exemplary—Wilke works within a feminist tradition that claims the aesthetic of idealization while simultaneously confronting a body's past, its changing present, and its specificity as the embodiment of a particular and singular individual woman.

But—I want to say. Is this the retrospectivity of a narrative whose ending we already know? What if, instead of documenting the seemingly brutal changes, both to her mother's and to her own body, Wilke had swerved away from self-representation at the moment when regimes of idealization were no longer efficacious? We are more accustomed to the self-representing beauties who, like feminine versions of both Narcissus and Echo (since they are both objects and producer/observers of their represented image), remain with us as youthful and beautiful, arrested by the equally traumatic events of early death or suicide. After all, how can one object to the narcissism of a young female artist who takes her life or whose life is taken from her when she is still the traditional culturally idealized image of beauty (I am thinking here especially of Mendieta and Francesca Woodman), early death being precisely what redeems her from the charge of "bad" narcissism, a narcissism that is too proud, too confident, and flaunts its disregard for what we think we know to be its eventual destination in bodily demise? Perhaps, then, we should understand this narcissism differently, as the obsessive recapturing of images of idealized beauty that bring together—too closely together, we might say for women artists in the western aesthetic tradition—the eye and the "I," the subject and the object, in defiant talking back to a cultural discourse that promises the punishment of withering away to every spring flower.

And what if one did not need to toughen up to look at these pictures, or what if one could lurk in the dark and arouse oneself to the moving images of *Through the Large Glass* without having

Intra-Venus #4, July 26, 1992–February 19, 1992

to confront the hag that always seems to emerge as the truth of the enchantress's surface beauty? That image, the enchantress turned hag, is a longstanding topos in western philosophy for the figure of truth—truth as woman, the truth of woman, woman as truth. Would the same critics, feminist or otherwise, praise the work of Hannah Wilke, or would we dismiss her? Is cancer scripted as the punishment for the narcissistic display of idealized beauty and youth?

I wish, somehow, we could tell this story backwards, I wish that once upon a time Hannah Wilke was a hag, or an ugly duckling, who documented the disfigurement of her youth but then, somehow, magically, miraculously, emerged in her fifties as a swan. Ah, but the ugly duckling is a story about a boy who becomes a man, a satisfyingly triumphant narrative about overcoming the odds to emerge maturely into beauty. Show me a story of a heterosexual woman that follows that path, that argues that the maturation of her body results in the magnificent splendor of the swan. You will remind me of the reality television show by that same name, *The Swan*, on which other papers in this collection will comment. But I would say that the goal there is to become other than who one is, to perfect through technology the imperfections of a nature that has somehow made a mistake. And is the story of (man's) artifice applied to nature to improve it (the very definition of art in the Renaissance, described by Alberti in *On Painting*) ever a story, for women, about organic maturation?[2] Is it ever a story about growing old?

If we were not reading retrospectively we might also pause to look at those images captured toward the end of Hannah Wilke's life. In some ways, those who praise the courage of those images also idealize, refusing in a way to look at them without the frame of a narrative of triumph in the face of disaster. If I try to see them this way (because of course we cannot exactly get out of the retrospectivity of our gazing), I think to myself, oh, she looks more like me there than she did "back then." She has heft, imperfection, beauty, all together. She is tired, playful, and the rigid anger is not so consistently present in her face and in the way she holds her pose. How might we look at her dying body in the present without the idealizing fantasies of heroism, courageous death, and survival against the odds?

Finally, though, and very personally—though in this personal meditation there may be something generalizable—what I would also like to learn from Hannah Wilke's work is how to banish envy, how to stop passing on the wound that seems to be one of the destinies of feminized women in the cultures of heteropatriarchy, whether it's the envy the old feel toward the young, the sick toward the well, or the always already de-idealized toward those who represent normative ideals. How to stop succumbing to the logics of exchange-value within which, Luce Irigaray once argued, "woman" circulates.[3] Wilke herself worked toward this goal in the portraits of herself with her mother and the portraits of older and dying women whom she loved. Likewise, how might we all acknowledge death—and the very impossibility of acknowledging death—so as not to hold to it like a punitive secret that will be revealed to those who are younger or still immersed in their immortality? So that, for example, the willowy, wonderfully formed young sarcastic in-your-face but very girly woman who was Hannah Wilke in her twenties might have had the chance to be celebrated, separately, differently, apart from and in addition to the woman who bravely, beautifully, ironically and, yes, also painfully, documented her bodily submission to death.

Notes

1. Joanna Frueh, *Hannah Wilke: A Retrospective* (Columbia, Missouri: University of Missouri Press, 1989), p. 44.

2. Leon Battista Alberti, *On Painting*, trans. Martin Kemp (London: Penguin Classics, 1991).

3. Luce Irigaray, *This Sex Which Is Not One*, trans. Catherine Porter with Carolyn Burke (Ithaca: Cornell University Press, 1985).

4

Beauty Loves Company

Joanna Frueh

I'm thinking these days that art is an offering of beauty: an offering to ourselves as sleeping beauties—beings who resist the beauty that we are. Awake, we are divine.

I'm thinking that Hannah Wilke both offered and attacked her own beauty—loved it and resisted it. While she modified the often culturally "uglified" female genitals in her numerous ceramic vulvas by maximizing their aesthetic value with playful colors and patterns, she also "scarred" her face and naked torso with vulval sculptures formed from chewing gum: representing herself as a woman damaged by female embodiment in a culture that subordinates woman to man. The "scars" simultaneously served as decoration, a metaphoric makeup adorned by woman in the martyrdom that some feminists, such as Sheila Jeffreys, perceive as femininity itself. In her recently published book *Beauty and Misogyny,* Jeffreys critiques Western beauty practices that she defines as harmful to women. The practices range from painting lips to shaving and waxing leg and pubic hair to wearing high heels to surgically altering labia, breasts, and feet, and all cause women to suffer physically—toxic chemicals in lipstick; bunions, hammer toes, and shortened calf muscles from too-small, too-tall shoes; surgeries that cut off women's body parts and cut up their skin. All the practices cause women emotional suffering too, in the very desire, which Jeffreys sees as a cultural imperative, to be beautiful and feminine, to be beautifully feminine—to mark oneself different from masculine man by acting properly submissive as a member of a gender underclass.

To suffer in any way is to suffer spiritually.

Wilke also depicted the divine Hannah. While she created herself as a thrilling icon of courage in self-portrait photographs taken near the end of her life, when she was experiencing cancer and its medical solutions, her self-creation as a model of pure beauty—heaven in the flesh—strikes me as her boldest artistic endeavor. For there, sculpted as a chocolate Venus or drawn as an angel, she modified the culturally damaged body of woman by picturing its divinity. I resonate to Wilke's self-loving art. She is my sister and my refreshment in a world whose disillusioned heart says ever so easily, Misery loves company. I say, Beauty loves company.

Divinity is palpable and invisible. It is the numinous world experienced and believed in by ancient, pagan cultures: the spirits met by Greeks in sacred groves; the jinn felt by Arabs in the desert; El, the epiphany of a pre-monotheistic Israelite god, the stranger with whom Jacob wrestled. Divinity points to Reality, which overwhelms theologians' abstract engagements in relations among God, the universe, and human beings, let alone those theologians' formulations of doctrine. Human beings have liked to admire divinity, and one display of that sensitivity to wonder is artists' creations of deities in human form. Hannah as angel and chocolate Venus personalized that wonder. The scholar of religion Karen Armstrong implicitly connects contemporary artists', poets' and musicians' symbolic representation of the divine with millennia-old beliefs. In her book *A History of God,* she explains how people of the ancient world most likely believed that they would become genuinely human only by engaging in the numinous. Wilke's *Venus Pareve,* sculpted of edible chocolate in the early 1980s, and her *Self-Portrait as Angel,* drawn in 1977, were not narcissistic aggrandizements, the self-portrait resulting from aggressive ego.

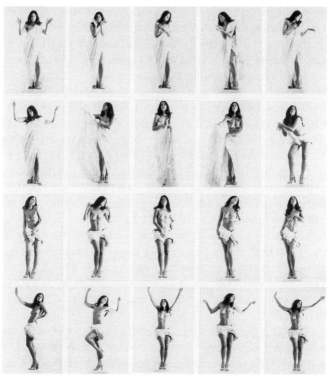

Super-t-Art, 1974

Angel and Venus say simply, I am who I am. And if divine form is human form, then divinity is human nature.

People spend a lot of time not being themselves. Conditioned by today's beauty idol, which is young, long-limbed, fair-skinned, and often blonde, big-bosomed, and blue-eyed, many women see and experience their appearance as inadequate and therefore in conflict with the idol. Rationally, women know that the beauty idol is, like any idol, a false notion that produces mistaken thinking. Yet the beauty idol, like any idol, garners ardent devotion—right now, from the fashion, beauty, and entertainment industries. They present the beauty idol as if it were real, so people mistake it for real, and in so doing create for themselves the intolerable situation of clothing beauty and themselves in illusions—beauty is beyond me and I am its contradiction. The title of a Derrick Jensen book, *The Culture of Make Believe*, published in 2002, comes to mind. Conditioned by an idol, we bathe and dress ourselves in make-believe—concepts cudgeled into us by a pictorial blast of generic bodies and faces. We are blinded by obedience to a corporate ideology, the current beauty idol that we let hide us from ourselves, that we let infantilize us into oblivion.

Idols are toys. The mind plays with them. The beauty idol is a toy that worries and disappoints us. We are children, frustrated and enraged by the toy that is a nightmare. Yet, we keep playing with it. For example, feminists keep writing about beauty as a problem—Jeffreys's 2005 publication is a case in point. We keep playing, because we are convinced, through our own suffering, that we must deal with what "is there." But the beauty idol exists through a perverse act of will: what we pay attention to becomes our reality, and our attention increases that reality.

Wilke gave herself wings. In *Self-Portrait as Angel* she wrote a dictionary definition of angel across her sacrum: **angel** 1. a spiritual being superior to man in power and intelligence 2. an attendant spirit or guardian 3. a winged figure of human form in fine art 4. a message originating from God in his aspects of truth and love.

I read the inscription on her sacrum, her sacred body/text as follows: woman is a spiritual being superior to man in power and intelligence; when human beings are open to the angels attending them, the human body is as beautiful as art; I, Hannah, am your attendant spirit, a guardian of your beauty, a messenger of truth and love.

Wilke gave herself sweetness. When I walked into her studio the first time, I smelled chocolate and wondered where the aroma was coming from. I turned around, to be surprised by a small band of foot-high Hannahs molded out of chocolate.

Wilke conceived herself as an ideal. The ideal of Beauty.

Increase, expansion, never-ending love. That is the infinite realm of Beauty.

In *Venus Pareve* and *Self-Portrait as Angel* she turned her attention to self-love. Thank you, Hannah, for increasing the reality that is Beauty by being yourself as you were, unconditioned by the beauty idol, unconditionally in love with yourself. Thank you for releasing the viewer from the conditioning that limits the mind in such a way that it attacks the body.

Tattoos, piercings, brandings, and surgical alterations of flesh perceived to be flabby and literally and figuratively fallen are images that come to mind when we think of contemporary Western practices of body modification. Often, people understand such body modification procedures to be painful—self-inflictions of suffering. Jeffreys stands in that camp. Those who have modified their bodies often see themselves as transgressive, and Jeffreys gives Shannon Bell's choice to be tattooed as an example. In "Tattooed: A Participant Observer's Exploration of Meaning," published in the *Journal of American Culture* in 1999, Bell observes her choice as a display of societal separation and a symbol of creativity. Modifications of the body modify a person's relation to society and her place within it.

Modifications of the body reflect modifications in the mind and spirit. We can be angels, we can be demons.

When the artist gives form to ideas, she can modify minds. An artist who images herself as Beauty sees heaven where most human beings see hell, having surrendered to a harrowing idea of beauty as diminishment. The fashion and medical industries manufacture beauty as an idol of decrease. Gray and silver are diminished into colorlessness by red, blonde, and brunette. Multiplicity of form is diminished by thinness. Diverse tonalities of skin are diminished by a glorified whiteness. Ages older than a Photoshopped or surgical smoothness are diminished by a homogeneous youthfulness. The diminishment of human being into a merciless idol of perfection dehumanizes beauty. Dehumanized, beauty becomes our demon.

Wilke played with her particularities. Light skin, narrow shoulders, brunette hair, small breasts, under-eye darkness and slender arms, wide hips, and unshaved underarms: some of those features fit a late twentieth-century and second millennium ideal, and some do not. In *Venus Pareve* and *Self-Portrait as Angel* the artist idealized those corporeal features. Such idealization is increase, expansion, never-ending love. In diminishment, we are strangers to ourselves, whereas in expansion we become our own intimate friend.

We learn diminishment by rote. It is a tedious and painful lesson memorized by the body's cells. We learn increase by heart, like a song we love to sing.

My heart hurt as I heard a woman obscurely addressing her own pain in a recent conference presentation about contemporary artists, such as Gina Pane, Marina Abramovic, and Orlan, whose bodies bled in their art works, from their own actions or from the artist's directions to others. Well into her performative lecture, the presenter, who now and then spoke in an obliquely personal manner, sat at a table, picked up a huge knife with her right hand, spread the fingers of her left hand on the table, and stabbed it between her digits, slowly at first and then faster. I looked away and when I looked back she was licking the blood from a finger that she had cut. Q & A followed her presentation, and I asked: "Do you think that people identify more with other people through pain or through pleasure?" She answered, "I don't know."

Wilke's chocolate and angelic pleasures welcome me. They permeate my cells.

Two days later at the conference I presented *The Performance of Pink*, in which my costume and my girly and romantic way with words and emotions activate the pleasure of pink, a color that lifts spirits and that symbolizes love. As is characteristic of my performances, the language and feeling of the piece is erotic. In a Q & A following the performance, a man asked, "What is your definition of 'erotic'?" I responded, "I see the erotic as connection," and as I spoke, the heart-hurting presentation entered my mind. I continued, "I see the erotic as positive connection, pleasurable connection, and I'm interested in the body of pleasure and an erotics of pleasure. An erotics of pain is abundant in our society. It bombards us, as does the body of pain." We are used to the body of pain, conditioned by an erotics of pain. The beauty idol is one instance of that body, and our suffering—as contradictions to that body—suffices as a strange erotics, an erotics of estrangement from the pleasure of increase and expansion.

At the same conference, technology and culture theorist Arthur Kroker gave a talk titled "Twisted Bodies." He spoke about the bodies of suicide bombers and their victims, about the horrific remains of 9/11 Twin Towers corpses—bits of skin, a finger, on the streets and sidewalks of New York. His words pictured idols fueled by contemporary fears of terrorist actions. After a while he said that he would speak about the body of pleasure. I imagined that it would radiate spirituality, but his words pictured cosmetic surgeries and other forms of what he termed "resurrection." I wrote in my conference schedule, addressing Kroker, "Your body of pleasure sounds like a body of pain," and his body of pleasure existed only as a material resurrection, which I interpret as a remodeling or a restoration.

I've heard that we come to know reality through contradiction—beauty and ugliness, pleasure and pain. Contradiction is the womb of conflict, and I've heard, too, that conflict is inevitable. Conflict, an inevitable reality. War in oneself over beauty and ugliness inevitable.

Wherever you see yourself is your reality.

When Wilke saw herself as beauty and pleasure in *Self-Portrait as Angel* and *Venus Pareve*, she untwisted the human body from the beauty idol's wringing grip. She rose from the deadness of artificial beauty into the realness of humility. In humility, a person feels no contradictions.

Humility is a state of balance. In his book *Humility*, a philosophical inquiry into the subject, Norvin Richards defines humility as a "matter of having oneself in perspective."[1] I see divinity as that perspective. St. John of the Cross, a Christian mystic who lived in sixteenth-century Spain, knew that in a state of humility, the spirit is neither pulled nor pushed, neither up nor down. At our center—in humility—we exist in a still joy. For the writer, political activist, and monk Thomas Merton, humility is a quality that makes human beings real.

Because we are awake.

When we are real, we do not resist ourselves, we are kind to ourselves. *Webster's New World College Dictionary* gives an archaic meaning of kind as "in agreement with one's . . . nature." Let human form and divine form agree with one another. And let us find ourselves . . . to be irresistible.

Note

1. Norvin Richards, *Humility* (Philadelphia: Temple University Press, 1992), p. xii.

II

Skin: Cosmetic Surgery and Tattooing

5

The Body, Beauty, and Psychosocial Power

Victoria Pitts

The authentic truth of a person, whether it is conceived as the inner self, the psyche, the soul, or identity is often thought to be visible on the body's surface. Multiple and contradictory interpretations of the relation of inner and outer selves of cosmetic surgery subjects have been offered in medical, psychiatric, political and popular discourses. My own project is to examine ways in which the normal and pathological subjects of cosmetic surgery are discursively and multiply produced; in doing this I hope to complicate current understandings of cosmetic surgery's power relations.

Visible Pathology

Cosmetic surgery has historically been seen as a corruption of the natural body-self relation. The body that has undergone cosmetic surgery has been criticized for creating an untruthful representation of the inner self, enabling it to pass as someone else. This was one of the moral objections that was made to cosmetic surgery in the nineteenth and early twentieth centuries, when it was seen as highly unnatural, not only because it involved technology and physical transformation, but also because it corrupted the normal, and even biologically driven coding of a person's character on the body. Historian Sander

Gilman describes how cosmetic surgery was feared for helping marginalized people pass into dominant groups, particularly disguising their race and their criminal tendencies. "One great social fear in early twentieth-century Europe and the United States," he writes, "was that the criminal, especially the Jew or black as criminal, would alter his appearance through the agency of the aesthetic surgeon and vanish into the crowd."[1] Such logic, of course, is highly essentialist—that is, it assumes that a person's essence is innate and authentic, fixed by race, ethnicity or some other category.

This essentialist logic still endures. We see it, for instance, in the relentless social fascination with Michael Jackson's racial transgression. As we can't help but be aware, Jackson has undergone a range of cosmetic procedures, achieving a face that looks much whiter, younger and more bizarre than might be expected. With his increasingly pale skin and thinning nose, Jackson is variously seen as post-Black, as a denier of his racial heritage, and—combined with his gender- and age-defying body modifications—as a freak. Jackson's exaggerated cosmetic alterations have become such a spectacle that it is difficult for us to avert our collective gaze. This is partly because he is seen as using technology to mask what we take to be his more authentic, biologically determined self, which would be Black, male, and, by now, middle-aged. The disruption of the apparently natural coding of the self (the gendered, racial self) onto the body is part of what ails Michael Jackson as a public figure, and thus what socially and politically perturbs us.

But while the surgically corrupted body may once have been seen as immoral, it is now also interpreted as pathological. Pathologizing discourses interpret the surgically transformed body as a record of symptoms of inner psychological disorder. Michael Jackson has been understood this way, as a person whose bodily surfaces indicate a disturbed inner self. For instance, as Nikki Sullivan suggests, Michael Jackson's cosmetic surgeries have been repeatedly analyzed in the media, where his face is interpreted by a range of experts. "Jackson's modified face is "read not only as the effect of an abusive childhood, but also as evidence of escalating psychological problems."[2] By repeatedly displaying images of his increasingly modified face as a visual illustration of his psychological biography, the media positions his physical transformation as indicative of increasing internal disorder. His face is interpreted as a version of his inner self, which can be read easily by experts, if not by the public at large. While his seemingly weird tastes and unorthodox attitudes and actions are also pathologized, the surface body is—tautologically—offered as the material evidence for pathology, which includes, at the very least, *cosmetic surgery addiction.*

Contemporary discourses about cosmetic surgery addiction expand this approach far beyond people whose body modifications are anomalous. Surgery addiction has recently been medicalized as a form of Body Dysmorphic Disorder (BDD), which has been listed in the Diagnostic and Statistical Manual of Mental Disorders since 1987, although many mental health professionals had not heard of it until recently.[3] People with BDD, it appears, will repeatedly seek out cosmetic surgery as a solution to psychic pain that reflects their obsession with perceived physical flaws. In the psychiatric literature, Body Dysmorphic Disorder is understood to be at least partially biological in origin and amenable to pharmacological treatment. Now BDD is being used to medicalize extreme cases of cosmetic surgery and to establish medical standards for patients' psychological attitudes toward their bodies.

Despite its fairly short history as an official psychiatric disorder, and the relatively few number of people actually diagnosed with it (the DSM estimates that between 1% and 2% of the population might have BDD, but the numbers of diagnosed people are far fewer), BDD has become a clinical buzzword in the current cosmetic surgery climate. This is partly due to the framing of BDD as a social problem in the media and partly due to the direct appeals psychiatrists have made to cosmetic surgeons to look for signs of the disorder in their patients. Prominent psychiatric experts in BDD, like Katharine Phillips and Raymond Dufresne, argue that cosmetic surgeons must try to detect it, not least of all because "patients with body dysmorphic disorder are also often dissatisfied with surgical treatment and may sue, threaten or even become violent toward the treating physician."[4] They argue that "it is better to over-diagnose than to under-diagnose" this disorder.[5]

The efforts to establish Body Dysmorphic Disorder as a recognized, legitimate diagnosis for "difficult" cosmetic patients are consistent with Peter Conrad and Joseph Schneider's description of the multi-staged medicalization process.[6] First, such behaviors are *already defined* as deviant in the public mind. In the case of BDD, psychiatrists do not need to convince people that undergoing cosmetic surgery—particularly multiple surgeries—should be considered suspect behavior, but rather that the behavior can be defined medically. Second, in *medical prospecting*, the behavior is found to be linked to some field of medicine by "describing research that creates such a link."[7] This process is being accomplished with BDD in part through the collection of case histories of possible BDD patients; through the retrospective application of the diagnosis to studies of cosmetic surgery and dermatology patients; through new psychiatric research of BDD patients; and through efforts to get cosmetic surgeons and dermatologists to use new screening techniques developed by psychiatrists. In the third step of medicalization, psychiatrists actively promote "the recognition of the problem in medical terms so that its discovery can be legitimated in the public arena."[8]

For its part, the media has busily speculated about the people who might have BDD. The DSM definition is often recited in media accounts, which emphasize that such a person has a distorted perception about an imagined or slight defect in appearance and that her or his life is significantly disrupted by a preoccupation with the perceived flaws. However, the disorder is also invoked even when symptoms that meet the diagnostic criteria for the disorder aren't apparent. For example, people who simply have had surgeries on multiple body parts are regularly cited as having the disorder in media accounts. In addition, people for whom appearance is said to be a minor distraction are sometimes described as having "mild" BDD, even though the DSM definition demands that a person experience significant distress or impairment in an important area of life functioning due to their appearance concerns. People with BDD are thought to be, like the rest of us, suffering from the effects of beauty culture, and the medicalized description is therefore set alongside the feminist beauty ideals theory of cosmetic surgery. A slippery slope is constructed that descends from vanity to mental illness. And although BDD is believed to be largely biological in origin, media accounts regularly link it to normal vanity, and the boundary between them is not very clear. From these accounts, one gets the impression that ordinarily vain people could find themselves having Body Dysmorphic Disorder if they are not careful. In other media descriptions, people who have spectacularly weird or abnormal tastes—like Michael Jackson and Jocelyne Wildenstein, the so-called "Cat Lady"—are invoked by journalists and the surgeons they interview as potential BDD sufferers. Unusual aesthetic tastes are problematized, as are unusual surgeries. Seemingly ordinary women who undergo unusual surgeries, like female genital cosmetic surgery, have been described as especially likely candidates for this diagnosis. Whatever the reality, the term has become a readily available code for any surgery or any patient that is considered "crazy," "disturbing," or "extreme."

In the past few years, BDD has been embraced in the cosmetic surgery discourse as a cognitive tool, clinical diagnosis, and media buzzword. I want to suggest that there are a number of structural and cultural reasons why this might be the case. First, psychiatry has achieved new prominence in its development of diagnostic categories that can quickly become recognizable and accepted.[9] The past thirty years have seen a significant development in the use of psychiatric drugs to treat mental suffering, an increased emphasis on evidence-based psychiatry and psychiatric diagnoses by health insurers, and the tripling of the number of official diagnoses in the DSM. The transformation of psychiatry influences the ease with which we adopt its diagnostic terms in public discourse in order to define (and even stimulate) social controversies. Second, there is an unprecedented explosion in the cosmetic surgery market, and for the first time we see widespread use of cosmetic surgery as well as many people getting multiple surgeries. Third, this explosion takes place in a society which is still ambivalent about cosmetic surgery, and which lacks any normative or regulatory certainty about how much surgery is enough and how much is too much. Fourth, there is relative silence from cosmetic surgery patients. For various reasons, many cosmetic surgery patients stay in the closet and have thus far let surgeons speak for them.[10] Their silence is compensated for by the media. Finally, there is enormous media interest in cosmetic surgery and BDD is operating as a lightning rod for social thinking about its problems.

There are some reasons to find this worrisome. I believe that there are serious implications for those who are pathologized. They become discredited persons, as the sociologist Erving Goffman would have described them.[11] A diagnosis of mental illness—or even the *suspicion* of mental illness—is often taken to be the defining feature of a subject's behavior, dwarfing other possible explanations. In practical terms, this means that patients' own perspectives on cosmetic surgery may be erased, and their own beliefs about surgery dismissed. Moreover, as a Foucaultian interpretation would emphasize, the effects of the diagnosis reverberate far beyond the specific individuals who might be diagnosed. The rise of BDD represents the normative power of psychiatric experts to foreground the individual's psyche as the primary public concern about cosmetic surgery, and to define acceptable modes of interiority in relation to body image and body modification.

"Becoming Surgical"

While many psychiatrists may privately oppose cosmetic surgery, the biologism and evidence-based emphases of psychiatry today render it neutral on its ethics and politics. It is individual patients, particularly those for whom cosmetic surgery is a solution to a specific, biologically rooted psychological problem, that are designated as pathological. This individualistic view is contradicted by feminist arguments against cosmetic surgery, most of which come under the rubric of the "beauty ideals" perspective. These arguments have identified cosmetic surgery as a particularly heinous outcome of beauty culture, which is the production of, and which works to affirm, oppressive cultural ideals of beauty that pressure women to think of themselves primarily in terms of their sexual appeal to men. This perspective indicts cosmetic surgery itself as politically problematic, and also judges women who use cosmetic surgery as having internalized oppression or "false consciousness."

I should point out that, although cosmetic surgery is rarely defended publicly by feminists, not all feminists are equally opposed to it. Some, like Kathy Davis, see women's surgeries as practices of relative choice and individual empowerment, thus establishing the "agency" side of the "agency-structure" debate that has been occupying feminist theory for a number of years. Yet the idea that women who get cosmetic surgery hate their bodies informs most published feminist critiques of the practice. Even Davis subscribes to this view. Although her defense of women patients has irritated some feminists, it hardly represents a resounding embrace of their mental health. Women aren't total dupes, according to Davis, but this "does not mean that I 'condone' the practice," she writes, "let alone the cultural norms that *make women hate their bodies* and want to have them altered."[12] Davis's sense of women's agency still depends on a context of women's enormous suffering. She suggests that when a woman becomes concerned with the appearance of her body, she experiences a downward spiral of "hopelessness, despair, and finally, resignation."

Ultimately, her body "becomes a prison from which there is no escape," except through cosmetic surgery.[13] This, please note, is coming from one of the more optimistic feminists writing on the subject.

I want to point out here that even in Davis's work, pathological and normal uses of cosmetic surgery are nearly impossible to distinguish from one another. Other writers—those who are more on the "structure" side of the debate—reject the distinction overtly. For example, Virginia Blum takes the view that nearly any cosmetic surgery is a coercive practice that preys upon people who are pathologically self-hating. She writes, "Just because culture has normalized our pathology . . . it doesn't mean that cosmetic surgery isn't like any other practice that has us offering up our bodies to the psychical intensities that angrily grip us."[14] In fact, she equates cosmetic surgery patients with people who have "delicate self-harm syndrome," a psychiatrically recognized mental illness that is mostly diagnosed in young women who repeatedly cut themselves. Blum asks: "How different is going under the knife in search of youth and beauty from some ritual and hidden adolescent cutting?"[15]

Although there are significant differences between feminist and psychiatric views of cosmetic surgery, radical feminists have offered arguments against cosmetic surgery that generally square with the psychiatric view on at least two points: first, that cosmetic surgery reveals something deep about the individual self and second, that what it reveals is pathological. Despite their rejection of psychiatry's biologism and its apolitical stance, radical feminists have applied the language of self-mutilation and addiction to women who choose to have cosmetic surgery. They have described such patients as sick women whose psyches have been rendered pathological by patriarchy.

There is an irony here that I am keen to point out. One of the reasons that feminists have historically been so opposed to cosmetic surgery is that it medicalizes norms of appearance. Kathryn Pauly Morgan has described beauty medicalization as the "double-pathologizing of women's bodies," since women's bodies have not only been treated as inferior in the histories of medicine, but are also being pressured to "achieve [beauty] perfection through technology."[16] This is so objectionable for feminists because when beauty is medicalized and defined by (male) experts, women's bodies are subjected to increased scrutiny and "treatment." Norms that vary historically (and are usually Eurocentric and heteronormative) are reified as natural and universal. But I want to argue that it is not only beauty that is now subject to medicalization in cosmetic surgery culture, but also *body image*—not only the outer body but the inner self. In this form of medicalization, beauty norms are much less relevant. It won't matter nearly as much now whether a woman's transformed body is meant to look normatively beautiful or horrific, gorgeous or transgressive. Its mere transformation will be seen as a sign of something important about the inner self that must be categorized diagnostically. (In fact, we saw precisely this in the pathologization of people with tattooed faces and pierced labia.)[17]

What the expansion of cosmetic surgery is now accomplishing, through the invocation of psychiatric diagnoses and ready pathologization, is the medicalization of women's attitudes about beauty on top of their actual bodily appearances. This could engender a much more totalizing medicalization of women's beauty than ever before (a "triple-pathologizing," in Morgan's terms), regulating both inside and outside, both surface and depth. Here, women's desires for bodily transformation, their goals and aims as well as their self-images, are defined by experts. If this form of medicalization is similar to previous versions, women's psyches will be scrutinized by experts and subjected to screening and treatment. Although the norms of body image vary historically, reigning norms will be reified as natural and universal. I am worried that the beauty ideals perspective, with its willingness to pathologize women who get cosmetic surgery, is inadequate to grasp this aspect of the power relations of medical beauty culture.

Good Candidates

The scenario I've just outlined is already happening. Concerns about surgery addiction and Body Dysmorphic Disorder, coupled with criticisms by psychiatrists and feminists about the psychological health of cosmetic surgery patients have caused the cosmetic surgery industry to sort cosmetic patients into "good" and "bad" surgical candidates. This includes the use of formal and informal screenings for BDD in cosmetic surgeons' offices.

In addition, the industry itself addresses the psychological dimension of cosmetic surgery with its promotion of an ideology of "cosmetic wellness," which defines cosmetic surgery as a self-care practice that lays "the groundwork for greater all-around health and well-being, as well as an enhanced ability to take control of one's life."[18] A person with a good self-image who cares about her well-being will not only get liposuction or a face lift when she "needs" it, therefore, but will stay fit, eat well, exercise and live life to the fullest. She might even treat depression or a problem with her body image surgically. The very "purpose of cosmetic surgery," says Dr. Gregory Borah, on behalf of the American Society for Aesthetic Plastic Surgery, "is to improve a person's psychological functioning by modifying their body image."[19]

As a result of this logic, cosmetic surgery has become an occasion for endless iterations of what constitutes the good patient, the good psyche, and the good body image. For instance, the American Society for Aesthetic Plastic Surgery, in the wake of public concern over BDD, has established an outline of how much cosmetic surgery a woman should get. "How much cosmetic surgery is too much?" asks the ASAPS.

> The answer depends on the reasons it is chosen, when it is chosen, and the patient's expectations. A patient who has a strong personal desire for self-improvement and is able to identify specific, realistic goals for surgery is likely to be a suitable candidate for one or more procedures.[20]

Lest we be uncertain about what those goals should be, the ASAPS published a timeline that identified what women's concerns might be at which age, and what cosmetic surgeries should be desired to address them. (Not surprisingly, it is a pretty expansive list.)

Clearly, the notion of cosmetic wellness appropriates liberal ideas of self-determination and agency. It also resonates with, and capitalizes on, the cultural prominence of ideas about healthy and empowered body-selves. The aim of cosmetic wellness includes a lifetime of body projects that reflect self-care, with the latter being determined by conceptions of the true inner self that should be explored, discovered, honored and expressed on and within the body. This notion of wellness, then, links cosmetic surgery to norms of the psyche: the proper body image, the right attitude, and the correct aims for cosmetic surgery. It brings together the seductiveness of desires for beauty, youth, and even empowerment with disciplinary discourses of right and proper selfhood. Further, it identifies body modification as a primary mode for articulating the authentic, healthy, and happy self.

This rhetoric not only reigns in cosmetic surgery clinics, but it also reaches the rest of us through the spectacles of cosmetic surgery that are now shown on television, where it is celebrated because it helps the body to express its "real" self. Take, for example, one of the participants of *Extreme Makeover*, Tess. A former beauty queen, Tess is a forty-four-year-old mother of three. She is said to have lost her looks to pregnancies and a cesarean operation. Through her visits to a cosmetic surgeon, dentist, and dermatologist, where she underwent multiple procedures costing tens of thousands of dollars, she purportedly regained "the beauty that once accompanied her indestructible spirit."[21] Her body had become, through life events and the passage of time (the gaining of weight and the bearing of babies), wrongly matched to its deep self. A beauty queen on the inside must look like one on the outside; a thin person is essentially one in the core of her being; an indestructible spirit must have an indestructible body. What cosmetic medicine does, then, is realign inner and outer selves, preserving the relationship between surface appearance and interior truth. More broadly, what this rhetoric also affirms is the role of the body in establishing and affirming identity.

The selves now promoted in cosmetic surgery culture are invested not only with the appeal of liberal notions of self-empowerment, but also with the values of multiculturalism and ethnic pride. The former beauty queen of *Extreme Makeover*, Tess is Filipino. For her facial surgery, *Extreme Makeover* did not use its usual cosmetic surgeons, but sought an expert in ethnic cosmetic surgery since—as the audience was told—Tess did not want to lose her ethnic identity through the surgical process. While the racialization of beauty has long been part of cosmetic surgery's history and the target of public criticism, now the promotion of "ethnically appropriate" surgery is informed by multiculturalism. Instead of aiming to erase racial difference, ethnically appropriate cosmetic surgery identifies differences in the needs and interests of racial and ethnic groups. Figuring out the variations among ethnic skin types in terms of likely reactions to surgery, lasers and other procedures is now part of cosmetic surgery research, and is seen as a quality of care matter among cosmetic surgeons.[22] But as the *Cosmetic Surgery Times* puts it, the "main caveats in these areas involve cultural features."[23] Such features include attitudes about eye shape among Asians, attitudes about noses among African Americans, Latinos' ideals of body shape, and so on. Ethnically targeted cosmetic surgery now aims to rethink Eurocentric beauty ideals in order to preserve the ethnic features of the person, and to "honor" her or his racial heritage.[24]

Such attempts may be welcome for some people of color who have been frustrated with the industry's homogenized view of beauty. But while "ethnically appropriate" cosmetic surgery might answer current bioethical criticisms about race and cosmetic surgery, it surely generates new ones. For instance, it reifies racial categories, universalizing beauty within ethnic groups and utilizing an essentialist logic that emphasizes innate rather than social meanings of race. It also demands that individuals see their "authentic" selves in racially or ethnically specific terms, which are themselves essentialized. More broadly, such logic affirms the accomplishments of postmodern consumer capitalism in establishing the proper relationship between the body and the self, where the body's role is to articulate the self's identity, appropriating multiculturalism to do so.

Inner Selves and Social Meanings

Cosmetic surgery not only creates a surface appearance that is normatively ideal, it also produces that appearance's psychic meanings. When Michael Jackson's face is read as a signifier of the true meaning of his inner self, it is decoded according to standards that are influenced by racialized, gendered norms of appearance. When he fails to look properly Black and middle-aged, Jackson is understood as a surgery addict and a sick person. Current trends in cosmetic surgery not only avoid the bizarre enfreakment that Jackson's extreme surgical project seems to effect; they also reject the entire history of racial passing in cosmetic surgery. A good candidate for cosmetic surgery these days will have a specific set of attitudes about such surgery, will undertake it for the right reasons at the right time, and will want to honor her authentic inner self, however that is defined. A bad candidate for cosmetic surgery will have the wrong attitude and the wrong reasons, will want to change the wrong body parts at the wrong times, and will want to erase her authentic identity. Thus, the dominant logics of contemporary cosmetic surgery now reach significantly beyond beauty ideals. They depend upon essentialist notions of authentic inner selves. They require an understanding of the body and its surface as a signifier of authentic inner meaning, and they recruit psychiatric strategies to decode the meanings they want to find.

My critical response to these logics is informed by post-essentialist, post-structural thought, particularly that of Michel

Foucault and Elizabeth Grosz. As Grosz argues, we should think of the psychic self as inscribed, just as we do the body. In her view, the body and embodied experience can be thought of as actively shaping the psyche as much they are shaped by it.[25] Grosz describes her approach as "a kind of turning inside out and outside in of the body." [26] She uses the metaphor of the Möbius strip to explain this view of the body-self: each feeds into the other and it is impossible to separate them or to identify a discrete originality in the outer body or the inner psyche. For Grosz, "people's experience of interiority is produced though the surface of the body, which we experience as already inscribed by cultural and social meanings of bodies that exist in social and cultural spaces."[27] In this post-essentialist view, neither psychic self nor physical body are fixed, natural or authentic, but rather continually created or in process.

One of the implications of a post-essentialist view is that discourses like psychiatry, which identify apparently fixed meanings for the self, have to be critically examined, as Michel Foucault has argued. From Foucault's perspective, we can see medicine and psychiatry as practices of social control that produce certain kinds of bodies and psyches.[28] Individual identities are shaped through the imposition of normative labels and categories, and bodies are made "docile" matter for the inculcation of social norms. In this sense, we can see cosmetic surgery as a disciplinary practice that medicalizes norms of beauty. Kathryn Pauly Morgan synthesizes a beauty ideals perspective with a Foucaultian analysis. She has argued that cosmetic surgery disciplines the body into and with beauty culture, creating docile bodies for cultural inscriptions that are underwritten with patriarchal and consumerist values. But a Foucaultian perspective does not permit us to ignore other ways in which the body-subject is disciplined. Psychiatric understandings about Body Dysmorphic Disorder also operate in disciplinary ways, defining what constitutes a healthy attitude about the body by identifying unhealthy or pathological positions. I see many feminist arguments as coercive in a similar way.

For Foucault, knowledge-power works through the dual mechanisms of visibility and articulability.[29] Visibility establishes what is seeable and why we see it and not something else. For instance, what is visible on the body—such as identity, pathology, health, wellness, or character—is historically shaped and, therefore, linked to social formations and forces. We might ask: How do such social developments as consumer capitalism, the rise of individualism, current conceptions of health and illness, and new configurations of medicine and technology influence what we see when we look at the body? And, further, what can be spoken about the body, about identity and the self? What statements can be made? As Foucault showed, fields of articulability are outlined by discursive systems like psychiatry and medicine. These are determining, and both order and have primacy over the visible. Visibilities do not "show up under light," but are "created by the light itself."[30] They are not created by discourse, therefore, but are inseparable from discursive conditions "which open them up."[31]

Following this reading of Foucault, I see the bodies of cosmetic surgery as sites of visibility where the self is exposed. But the selves we see, and how we speak about them, are far from fixed. They are pathological, but also well. They are self-destructive, but also identity affirming. They are in touch with themselves and out of touch, inauthentic and authentic, extreme and normal. Thus, the psychic and bodily inscriptions that in Grosz's view are co-constituted are not univocal and singular, but multiple and contradictory. The meanings of the body and self are inter-subjective rather than interior; they are produced rather than simply expressed; they are in process rather than fixed or authentic.

Referring to psychotherapeutic and radical feminist inter-pretations of the sickness of cosmetic surgery patients, Sullivan argues that these perspectives assume that the meanings of body practices lie within the subject, in his or her "psychosomatic history," rather than in inter-subjectivity, social context and interpretation. But in Sullivan's account of Michael Jackson, the significant meanings of his modified face do not derive simply from some inner essence of self that he is expressing. They are also outside of Michael Jackson: for instance, in the social relations of psychiatry and psychology that use Jackson's body to generate knowledge about his psyche; in related feminist treatments of body modifiers as self-mutilators; and in the entertainment media, which presents Michael Jackson's body over and over again for spectacle. In this reading, it is not Michael Jackson whom we should try to make sense of, but our fascination with him.

In my own account of cosmetic surgery, I find multiple ways in which we look to the intentions and psychosomatic history of the individual subject in order to generate its meanings. Some have searched for the deep psychic pathologies behind cosmetic surgery—its link to psychoanalytic problems, personal pathologies, and diagnosable psychiatric disorders. In this vein, we have heard that cosmetic surgery is good for the self, as a cure for stigma and inferiority complex, and also that it is bad for the self, because it indulges body image disorders. Feminists have looked for signs of internalized political oppression and gendered self-hatred. Surgeons have made their own observations about cosmetic surgery patients, and have recently been asked to screen them, identifying predictable, reliable ways to delineate good and bad patients. In turn, they have generated distinctions between good and bad reasons and right and proper timelines for cosmetic surgery, and they have articulated the kind of body-self attitude that a patient ought to have. Medical researchers championing ethnically appropriate cosmetic surgery are now looking for the "true" beauty ideals that ought to be matched with ethnic identity.

These efforts try to decode the body as a signifier of the psyche. But are cosmetic surgery's meaning and significance really found in the normalcy or pathology of the individual person? Feminists have always been wary of the individualizing moves of psychiatry, but I want to push our feminist response further. I want to turn cosmetic surgery's meanings inside out, and argue that the interior meanings of cosmetic surgery are being inscribed on the bodies of people who get cosmetic surgery as much as their bodies are inscribed by their inner meanings. In suggesting this, I am claiming that the cosmetic surgery junkie is produced by the industry's practices and its political and cultural economy, as much as it is by the individual, pathological psyche. This doesn't mean that surgery obsession doesn't exist, but it means that its very definition is a matter of social judgment. Alongside the surgery junkie, cosmetic surgery culture is also creating the "good" surgery patient. But I want to see normal cosmetic surgery not as the result of choice, rationality, reason and restraint, and not as a choice by a sane patient who has the right and proper body image, as cosmetic surgery interests suggest. Instead, the normal cosmetic surgery patient is as much of a construction as the abnormal patient. Both are being produced by recent shifts in medicine, embodiment, and consumption, which convince us of new values and norms that influence our desires for body transformation and self-expression.

Foucault's analysis pushes us far beyond questions of whether or not cosmetic surgery is good or bad, or whether cosmetic surgery patients are healthy or sick. Foucault intends us to inquire about the epistemological basis of these questions. In this spirit, I do not mean to suggest that personal, psychic meanings of the body are not important, and that they are not relevant in our consideration of the ethics of cosmetic surgery. But I would argue that our attempts to extract and decipher these meanings reveal at least as much about our social norms and instruments of understanding as they do about individual truths. I would argue further that they code the psyche as much as they decode the body. As Gilles Deleuze says, following Foucault, "truths are inseparable from the procedure establishing it."[32] We should not receive these truths uncritically.

Notes

1. Sander Gilman, *Making the Body Beautiful: A Cultural History of Aesthetic Surgery* (Princeton: Princeton University Press, 1999), p. 27.

2. Nikki Sullivan, "'It's as Plain as the Nose on his Face': Michael Jackson, Modificatory Practices, and the Question of Ethics," *SCAN: Journal of Media, Culture, Arts* 1, no. 3 (2004), scan.net.au.

3. Katharine A. Phillips. *The Broken Mirror: Understanding and Treating Body Dysmorphic Disorder* (Oxford: Oxford University Press, 1998).

4. Raymond Dufresne et al., "A Screening Questionnaire for Body Dysmorphic Disorder in a Cosmetic Dermatology Surgery Practice," *American Society for Dermatologic Surgery* 27 (2001): pp. 457–462, 457.

5. *Ibid.*, p. 458.

6. Peter Conrad and Joseph Schneider, *Deviance and Medicalization: From Badness to Sickness* (Philadelphia: Temple University Press, 2000).

7. Mark Tausig, Janet Michello and Sree Subedi, *A Sociology of Mental Illness* (Upper Saddle River, New Jersey: Pearson/Prentice, 2004), San Francisco, p. 155.

8. *Ibid.*

9. Peter Conrad, "The Shifting Engines of Medicalization" (2004 Leo Reeder Award Lecture, presented at the American Sociological Association, San Francisco, Aug, 16, 2004).

10. Kathy Davis, *Dubious Inequalities and Embodied Differences: Cultural Studies on Cosmetic Surgery* (Lanham, Maryland: Rowman and Littlefield, 2003).

11. Erving Goffman, *Stigma: Notes on the Management of Spoiled Identity* (New York: Simon and Schuster, 1963).

12. Davis, 2003: p. 14.

13. *Ibid.*

14. Virginia Blum, *Flesh Wounds: The Culture of Cosmetic Surgery* (Berkeley: University of California Press, 2003), p. 289.

15. *Ibid.*

16. Kathryn Pauly Morgan, "Women and the Knife: Cosmetic Surgery and the Colonization of Women's Bodies," in *The Politics of Women's Bodies,* ed. Rose Weitz (Oxford: Oxford University Press, 1998), pp. 147–163.

17. Victoria Pitts, *In the Flesh: The Cultural Politics of Body Modification* (New York: Palgrave, 2003).

18. Michelle Copeland, *Change Your Looks, Change Your Life* (New York: Harper Collins, 2003), p. 38.

19. ASAPS press release, "Psychological Impact: Cosmetic Surgery Improves Quality of Life," May 2, 1997.

20. ASAPS press release, "'Excessive' Cosmetic Plastic Surgery: How Much is Too Much?" Feb. 27, 2004.

21. *Extreme Makeover*, ABC, www.extrememakeover.com.

22. Harry E. Pierce, "Cosmetic Surgery of Black Skin," *Dermatologic Clinics* 6 no. 3 (1988): pp. 377–385, 383.

23. John Jesitus, "Ethnic skin: handle with care: dark skin is more protected from sun, but vulnerable to hyperpigmentation, scarring," *Cosmetic Surgery Times*, June (2004), www.cosmeticsurgerytimes.com.

24. Kimberly Leydig, "Cosmetic Changes," Outlook XLI, no. 1 (2004), medschool.wustl.edu/~wumpa/outlook.

25. Elizabeth Grosz, *Volatile Bodies: Toward a Corporeal Feminism* (Bloomington: Indiana University Press, 1994).

26. Elizabeth Grosz, "Bodies-Cities," in *Feminist Theory and the Body: A Reader*, eds. Janet Price and Margrit Shildrick (New York: Routledge, pp. 381–387).

27. Laura Mamo and Jennifer Ruth Fosket, "Scripting the Body: Pharmaceuticals and the (re)Making of Menstruation," (paper presented to the American Sociological Association, Philadelphia, August, 2004), p. 14.

28. Foucault, Michel. *Birth of the Clinic: An Archaeology of Medical Perception* (New York: Vintage Books, 1994 [1973]).

29. Gilles Deleuze, *Foucault* (London: Continuum, 1988).

30. *Ibid.*, p. 52.

31. *Ibid.*, p. 57.

32. *Ibid.*, p. 63.

6

Love My Neighbor,
Hate Myself:
The Vicissitudes of Affect
in Cosmetic Surgery

Virginia L. Blum

ABC's reality makeover hit, *Extreme Makeover,* surprised everyone, including the network. Originally intended to be a one-off series aired in fall 2002, *Extreme Makeover* created such a sensation that it soon became a staple of ABC's Thursday night reality programming lineup. This extraordinary series features "everyday people" (often expressly identified as working-class) who undergo radical or extreme revisions to their physical appearance. The show's producers choose from an applicant pool based on a number of criteria, including the viability of the procedures candidates request and their presumed psychological health.[1] Typically, the extreme makeover entails a range of interventions on the part of plastic surgeons, cosmetic dentists, dermatologists and even ophthalmologists. Their physical transformations are followed up by the less invasive and more conventional makeovers of workout regimes, hair style and color, makeup and wardrobe. This makeover plastic surgery series was swiftly followed by many others including *The Swan, I Want a Famous Face, Plastic Surgery Before and After, Beverly*

Hills Plastic Surgeon, and *Dr. 90210*—indeed, we seem to have a unappeasable appetite for stories of surgical rescue stories.

In order for cosmetic surgery (traditionally seen as a hyper-investment in appearance over substance) to have gone so mainstream, certain conventional cultural values had to be recruited on behalf of representing these surgeries not as vain and superficial but as a route toward glowing self-improvement, not as acts of self-loathing but evidence of self-esteem, and the patients not as passive victims of consumer beauty culture but as take-charge agents eager to author their lives. Cosmetic surgery is no longer dismissed as a silly and imprudent waste of money, but is now condoned as an investment in your future; nor is it the elite purview of the rich and celebrated, but rather (and this is central to the whole industry) a deeply democratizing option. Just as the *Bachelor* and *Bachelorette* series have both reacted to and participated in carving out mainstream cultural fantasies about soul mates and emotional connections, and just as the Survivor series has specialized in distilling resourcefulness in a state of nature, plastic surgery makeover programming latches onto to a set of widely held American identity motifs that manage to offset the equally widely held negative assessments of both the practice and the kinds of people who could possibly engage in it.

Television is normalizing plastic surgery in US culture in stages. Once relegated to the "special" or exposé or talk-show revelation or even medical channel documentary, cosmetic surgery now occupies primetime in mid-stride from being outrageous to everyday. Just to offer a sense of how rapidly this normalization process is taking place, consider the following: In a *New York Times* article entitled "How Young Is Too Young to Have a Nose Job and Breast Implants?" the reporter writes the following: "The teenagers were notably realistic in their assessments of the body part they wanted to have changed . . . . Rather than overestimating their physical problem, they typically rated their deformity as less severe than the surgeons did."[2] In other words, the teenager's internalization of what

Naomi Wolf once pathologized as the "beauty myth" now renders her an apparently healthy member of the culture.[3]

Extreme Makeover is simply one among many makeover programs. On television, and in reality programming as well, it's "normal" to want to look buff and beautiful, normal within the terms of the understood contract between viewers and producers regarding what can and cannot appear within the televisual setting. Indeed, where better to become beautiful but on the air—and thus wonderfully the television, the social site *par excellence* for the experienced insufficiency of the masses, turns into a benefactor, while viewers are encouraged to identify as the potential beneficiaries of television's deep commitment to our self-improvement. This constitutes an ethical transposition whereby plastic surgery, which was until recently widely deplored as a practice dwelling on the superficial and inauthentic, is now increasingly embraced as central to values promoting well being and happiness. Such a transposition happens, I will argue, in part through the reversal of negative affect (or self-loathing) into its apparent opposite—self-love. Moreover, the makeover program's sudden and radical conversion of attacks against the ego into what feels ego-strengthening leads to an intoxicating postoperative experience (the bandages-off moment). This moment is further intensified by its having become a cultural trope.

The participants in *Extreme Makeover* already know exactly what is wrong with them. These ordinary people bring to the plastic surgeons a veritable menu of their surgical requests. The surgeons seem to generously mirror the patients' expectations with a surgical aesthetic that already had been internalized by their patients. The surgeons will confirm the patient's sense of inadequacy (which is inevitably shaming) and yet almost instantly reassure the patient through the promise that they will transform what is ugly and insufficient into what is beautiful. Importantly, because the patients already know what they want, the surgeons appear to serve the patients' best interest. In contrast to representations of surgeons as predators who manipulate the insecurities of (largely) women in order to pay off their mortgages and their children's college tuitions, here they are kindly healers—carefully attending to that delicate combination of wounded bodies and psyches.

During the first two series of *Extreme Makeover* the doctors, trainers, and style consultants all changed weekly. By its second year, however, every week we started seeing the same surgeons, the same dentist and dermatologist, and the same fashion consultant and trainer. Indeed, the opening credits of the program became reminiscent of the opening credits of another makeover show on Bravo, *Queer Eye for the Straight Guy*. Like *Queer Eye*'s "Fab Five," Extreme Makeover refers to its "extreme team." These are surrogate and provisional makeover families in the business of counteracting the shame and degradation set up by the structure of the makeover program itself, especially when it involves the body. Makeover programming subjects need to be rescued from their ugly and disorganized lives, their bad taste and miserable looks, sutured into the glad and radiant world. The makeover team thus becomes a temporary caregiving unit that may indeed humiliate one, but since we know that in the end they will love us and care for us and correct our deficits, they appear to undo the very shame that their presence in our life occasions.

I Want a Famous Face

Like other reality programs, *Extreme Makeover* charts the progress of becoming-celebrity. Ordinary people are suddenly stars—not only in physical appearance but also in the media coverage they receive as a result of appearing on these reality programs. *Extreme Makeover* shows us people being made good-looking enough to be on television; it is, in other words, a kind of ground zero of celebrity-building.

Not long after *Extreme Makeover* first aired, MTV gave us *I Want a Famous Face*, which differs from its predecessor in significant ways. Organized around the stories of largely very young people who want surgery to transform their faces or bodies in the image of a favorite celebrity, *I Want a Famous Face* is more critical of plastic surgery culture. The producers don't pay for the surgeries, they depict the surgery itself as well as its aftermath more graphically, and they typically incorporate in each episode negative experiences with plastic surgery, such as botched breast implants. Repeatedly, the participants on *I Want a Famous Face* express their conviction that these changes will improve their lives—either they'll become stars themselves or, like one Ricky Martin wannabe, they hope to win the heart of someone they secretly adore.

Typically, the young participants on *I Want a Famous Face* bring to the surgeons pictures of what they're after and the surgeons more often than not promise them a match. Each episode concludes with either a photo shoot or some other quasi–star turn that confirms the identification with the star template. What these individuals may hope to achieve through surgery is complicated. Stars' beautiful appearance can begin to seem like both cause and effect of their exquisite material lives. Much more than *Extreme Makeover, I Want A Famous Face* underscores the self-loathing of the young people pursuing surgery; although most of them are conventionally attractive to begin with, we learn in painful detail how inadequate they feel in relation to their template celebrity, whose imagined share of universal love (the love that is celebrity's cultural due) they cheerfully label "self-esteem."

From a psychoanalytic perspective the ease with which self-loathing gets reversed into the appearance of self-esteem is unsurprising. In the event of one reversal into its opposite in a dream, Freud observed, one should be on the lookout for other such reversals.[4] In *Civilization and Its Discontents*, Freud discusses at length one of the central affective reversals of civilization, the commandment to love one's neighbor as one loves oneself—which, as he notes, "cannot be recommended as reasonable . . . . Not merely is this stranger in general unworthy of my love; I must honestly confess that he has more claims to my hostility and even my hatred."[5] Freud ultimately argues that it is precisely because our innate aggressivity threatens to undo all the ties that bind of civilization that we must erect into a central tenet of human relationships this improbable formula. In his seminar on *The Ethics of Psychoanalysis* Jacques Lacan focuses on the role identification plays, not only in the aggressive relationship among human beings, but more importantly in producing subjects in endless conflict with ourselves. Lacan's account of subject formation involves visual identifications with other human objects which plunge the subject into an ongoing structural rivalry with an ideal who is simultaneously external and internal; he points out that to love one's neighbor as one loves oneself is easy enough when one considers that this so-called neighbor is no more than the "other" constitutive of the ego. As he put is it, this is "the most neighborly of neighbors who is inside me."[6] Cosmetic surgery thus holds out the uncanny capacity to transform into material reality the subject's complicated identifications, that always involve simultaneously the idealizations of love and the equally intense experience of rivalry.

The viewer of the surgical makeover program, who identifies with this radical shift in affect on the part of the patient, experiences gratification through the ways in which our aggressivity (directed at the original "ugly" patient) is transformed into our putative good will (our feelings of joy as a consequence their successful makeover). That cosmetic surgery is marketed as among the ultimate achievements of modern civilization is ironic, in light of the war it depicts between those counterforces of primitive destructiveness and the injunction to love our neighbor.

Finally, it is this discourse of self-improvement plundering feelings of self-loathing that is ethically squaring plastic surgery with mainstream American practices and values. Surgeons correct perceived mismatches between insides and outsides, adrenalize self-esteem, give aging businessmen a fighting chance in a youth-saturated market, urge that former wallflower to shine at her class reunion, rescue aging housewives from their cruel dowdiness. Surgeons urge us forward into our self-determined corporeal destinies. Ultimately, they promise to make us love-worthy—to the neighbor who is ourself. Those final moments of *Extreme Makeover*, when the patients are returned by their temporary caregiving family to their "real" friends and family—are no less than celebrations of their new love-worthiness—a love-worthiness achieved through vivid acts of self-hatred. What apparently rendered one unloveable, one's appearance, is now transformed into the very source of pleasure as the patient achieves (and the spectator witnesses) those twin poles of American desire, youth and beauty. Ideological conversions yoked to affective conversions makes cosmetic surgery an especially compelling story right now. More, as the distance increasingly narrows between unattractiveness and its "cure," as cosmetic surgery becomes more widely available both economically and ideologically to the middle classes, it will become a less interesting story precisely because the body that diverges from conventional attractiveness will no longer be perceived as at risk—given the high probability that the imperfect feature will be corrected in no time at all.

Notes

1. Participants need to be healed in time for their celebratory "reveal."

2. Mary Duenwald, "How Young Is Too Young to Have a Nose Job and Breast Implants?" *New York Times*, Sept. 28, 2004, The Consumer section.

3. Naomi Wolf, *The Beauty Myth: How Images of Beauty Are Used Against Women* (New York: William Morrow & Co., 1991).

4. Sigmund Freud, *The Interpretation of Dreams* in *The Standard Edition of the Complete Psychological Works of Sigmund Freud*, vol. 4, ed. James Strachey (London: Hogarth, 1900), p. 288.

5. Sigmund Freud, *Civilization and Its Discontents* in *SE*, vol. 21 (ed. James Strachey, London: Hogarth, 1927–1931), p. 110.

6. Jacques Lacan, *The Ethics of Psychoanalysis, Book 7, 1959–1960.* (ed. Jacques Alain-Miller, trans. Dennis Porter, New York: Norton, 1986), p. 187.

7

Embodied Subjectivity and the Quest for "Self" in Televised Narratives of Body Modification

Maria Frangos

Over the past couple of years, there has been a proliferation of documentary-style television shows that tell the stories of people's body modifications by means of surgery and other medical procedures. Here I will concentrate on three specific kinds of body modification narratives. The first is the full-body surgical beauty makeover performed upon the female contestants on the very popular Fox Television series *The Swan*.[1] In brief, each week on the hour-long show, the camera follows, in documentary style, two contestants (yes, it is a competitive reality show) who are evaluated by a team of surgeons and beauty "experts" and found sorely lacking in many ways. The experts determine what procedures are needed to make the woman (the ugly duckling) into a beauty pageant contestant (the swan). The procedures are then performed—and can include, for example, a tummy tuck, breast lift and/or implants, liposuction, nose reshaping, calf, cheekbone, or buttock implants, tooth veneers or in some cases extensive dental surgery, diet, intense workout regimen, and of course, "counseling," an attempt to tackle any self-esteem problems that may have emerged as a result of her deficiency of beauty. At the end of each show, there is a dramatic "reveal," where each contestant dazzles the audience, the host, their team of surgeons, and their families and friends with their transformation. One contestant is selected from the pair to move on to the "Swan Pageant"—the show's season finale— where one person is selected to be crowned "The Swan."

The other two types of narratives I will talk about here are from slightly less popular—but still ubiquitous—documentary-style shows found on the Discovery Channel and The Learning Channel, as well as on their various spinoffs, such as Discovery Health. These shows have much more of a traditional documentary feel to them—there is no contest, no dramatic reveal, although we are witness, reality-show style, to the actual surgeries. These narratives introduce us to the subjects of the transformations. They are interviewed by the camera about their lives, they go about their daily routines, we meet their families and friends—at least, those who are willing to be interviewed— and we hear stories about their childhoods, with accompanying voiceover speculations about the connections between their early family experiences and their desire for surgical modification. In this Discovery Channel style of narrative, the two kinds of body modification that are dealt with are transformation of sex and transformation of species. In *Changing Sexes: Female to Male* and its accompanying *Male to Female*, we are introduced to three subjects in each show who are seeking sex reassignment surgery or treatment. In *Humanimals: Wild Makeovers*, we meet several people who have chosen to have their bodies surgically modified so that they more closely resemble the creature from the animal kingdom with whom they identify.

What is interesting and important about these three kinds of popular television narratives are the different ways they construct the subjectivities of their participants, depending on the kind of modification that is being dramatized. I would like to consider how these narratives engage with and complicate the idea of self—specifically, the idea of self as other, and of other as self. In *Second Skins: The Body Narratives of Transsexuality,* Jay Prosser suggests that "the resexing of the transsexual body is made possible through narrativization, the transitions of sex enabled by those of narrative."[2] Extending his point to include many other forms of bodily transformation, I would argue that the transition from ugly duckling to swan, from a reviled physical self to a desired ideal, is also enabled by the twists, turns, and transitions that narrativization produces. The metamorphoses of these subjects are due not only to surgeries and other technologies of transformation, but also to the ways that their stories are told—the ways that the subjects themselves tell their own stories, and the ways the stories are told for them, on their behalf. The particular narrative "turn" I will concentrate on here is the turn from self to other—or from other to self—that is the arrived-at and celebrated narrative telos.

At the dramatic moment of the "reveal" on *The Swan,* each contestant comes out and stands before a huge curtain—behind which is hidden a full-length mirror. Each signals when she is "ready" for the curtain to be lifted and, when they see their new bodies for the first time, all speak the same sentence, week after week: "I'm not myself at all!" or, "I don't look like me at all!" And, of course, they are very happy about this—it is clearly a cry of joy they utter in these moments before the mirror. They are happy that their physical beings no longer reflect that which they have come to identify as their "selves." As soon as the "unattractive" body parts are gone or changed, the "self," the "me" of these women is gone as well.

When these women say "I am not myself," it is as though they have no "interiority"—their "selves" cannot be considered "interior," because their senses of self seem to be completely derived from their exteriority. For them, "me," "myself," is, and can only be, the crooked teeth, the "excess" weight, the unsatisfactory nose, the too-small or too-droopy breasts. This brings to mind Freud's bodily ego and Didier Anzieu's concept of the skin ego, where the "self"—the ego—is determined, formed, by the state of the body's exterior, particularly the skin. For Anzieu, the body is both the same as its mental projection and responsible for producing that projection.[3] This idea has been taken up by theorists to discuss the experience of transsexuality, but I find it especially useful in thinking about how the *Swan* contestants' senses of self are determined by their exterior appearance while the transsexual sense of self, as it is narrated on the Discovery Channel documentaries, is not.

Also, and very importantly, the *Swan* contestants do not provide narratives of "being." Theirs are narratives of negation with an emphasis on lack and incompleteness. Because of a deficiency of beauty, they were not capable of being what they wanted to be. For this reason, they are characterized through a discussion of what they are *not*: feminine, confident, social, charming, sometimes even good wives or mothers.

The narratives of sex transformation deal with the idea of self in relation to the body in a very different way. The *Female to Male* documentary introduces us to three subjects who are planning sex reassignment surgery—Rachel, who is planning to have her breasts removed first, and later have testosterone therapy, and who will change her name to Ryan; Dirk, formerly Emily, who is currently taking testosterone and who is saving up enough money to have his breasts removed, and Scott; who has had testosterone therapy, his breasts removed, and has also had a phalloplasty.

The narratives of those seeking transsexual body modification represent more positive and active subjects than the narratives of women who want to become more beautiful. Despite their female sex and female bodies, the female-to-male transsexuals are depicted through narratives of "being," of having *been* masculine. Their narratives suggest that, from birth, they "were" male, they "were" tomboys, they "were" athletic. Rachel played with GI Joes while her identical twin sister played with dolls; young Emily was more interested in catching bugs and fish than we are supposed to think "normally" sexed little girls should be. We are told that, from the very beginning, something was decidedly "off," and needed correction. In the way that their stories are told, the sex-change subjects compel the viewer to believe that they were already able to "be" what they wanted to "be" before and without the surgery; that surgery really has no effect on the interior self, which is always already male. Surgery simply fixes aspects of the material body that are "only skin deep,"—so that the physical self can pass in the outside world. One of the transsexual subjects, Rachel, soon to be Ryan, comments, after she has gone through the first phase of her transformation, breast removal: "When I look at myself in the mirror, it's how I've always seen myself."[4] This is why they assert, after their procedures are complete, that they are finally completely themselves—the opposite declaration from that of the *Swan* contestants ("I am finally no longer myself"). As the female narrator of this documentary states, "for most transsexuals, being true to one*self* means changing one's body."

Of course, one important difference between these two kinds of narratives of body modification is that there is a set of medical and psychiatric discourses shaping and determining the way transsexual subjects narrate their senses of self. These discourses are rooted first in nineteenth- and early twentieth-century sexology with their discussions of the sexual "invert," who experienced a disjunction between his sexed body and his perceived interior gender. This image of one gender "inside" in contrast to a different sexed "outside" bore a clear resemblance to narratives of transsexuality, and persisted as a way to describe transsexual subjectivity. So there is a reason for and a history behind this discourse of transsexuality, of a self inside at odds with the body. What is interesting, though, is why other forms of body modification that revolve intensely around a concept and image of the self—the Swan narratives—don't operate similarly. One might just as easily say, "my true self, inside, is beautiful, and now the outside matches"—which is something we have heard, for example, in Victoria Pitts's discussion of Tess, a participant on *Extreme Makeover*. But that is not the way it is usually expressed by these contestants on *The Swan*.

What does it mean that these televised narratives of physical transformation give us a feminine sense of self that is only formed from the outside in, and a male/masculine sense of self that is formed from the inside out?

When thinking about this question, it is important to remember that both narratives of transformation are narratives of improvement. *The Swan* narratives are quite transparently so. But the transformations from female to male are also; not only in the sense that the subjects of the modifications will experience the interior self and the body as finally aligned, but also in the sense that, in this culture, femaleness *is* a flaw or defect, and the transformation from female into male is a narrative of progress, of perfection. Think, for example, of Loren Cameron's book, *Body Alchemy*, where the turn, the transition, from female to male is figured as alchemy, the metallurgical art practiced by magi in the middle ages wherein a base metal—for Cameron, the female body—is transformed into gold—the male body. Or, think of how numerous the accounts are of females transforming into males in early modern literature, but how few if any there are that represent the opposite process. As the sixteenth-century French surgeon Ambroise Paré explains, "we therefore never find in a true story that any man ever became a woman, because Nature tends always toward what is most perfect and not, on the contrary, to perform in such a way that what is perfect should become imperfect."[5]

So both shows give us narratives of improvement for the female body—one option for the imperfect female body is heightened feminization and beautification, while the other option for improvement is to render the body male, which can only be done if the sense of self was always already male.

Changing Sexes: Male to Female, the sex-change documentary's companion show, might shed some light on how gender functions in the production of a sense of self that is rooted in the body. Here much of the narrative is similar to the *Female to Male* version, as is the idea of seeking body modification in order to make the outside reflect a preexisting gendered interiority. What is different is the way the interior gendered self is characterized. Unlike the female-to-male transsexual narratives, these narratives focus on the many small details that must be mastered by those who seek to be physically transformed into women. Although the male-born subjects of the documentary describe early feelings in childhood of being more comfortable in girls' clothes, or playing with girls' toys, they are also shown undergoing training with a consultant in San Francisco whose job it is to teach them how to be feminine—how to walk, how to sit and stand, how to make hand gestures that appear more female than male. The interior male selves of female-to-male subjects seem able to triumph over anything other than the physical matter of the body. Their gestures were always already male, their walk was always already masculine, they were always already athletic and "manly" in their pursuits. But the interior female self of the male-to-female subject cannot overcome the power of the male sexed and gendered body to give her pre- or post-transformation self the female stance, gestures, and physical bearing that she desires.[6]

Why this difference between the two? Does this have something to do with the female sense of self being produced from the outside in these narratives, and the male sense of self emanating from the inside? It is my argument that the two are connected, and I would like to consider the possible consequences of these very popular narratives presenting us with a female or feminine sense of gendered self that is more exterior than a male or masculine one. First, it threatens to return us to the timeworn trope of femaleness or femininity as artifice, and maleness, or masculinity, as somehow a purer, more organic expression of gendered being. It also presents us with more complicated questions about gender and the perception of the self. Does the sex-change subject's strong interior subjectivity mean that, when harmony is achieved, identification between inner and outer self is more tightly sutured than it is for others? Does it mean that that this identification might be more tightly sutured for female-to-male transsexuals than for male-to-female trans people?

And, if one's sense of (feminine) gendered self is completely exterior, is it possible that there is room for something to remain—as part of subjectivity—that might not participate completely in the regime of gender? How would one articulate this, when there really is no discourse for an incomplete identification with one's own gendered self that is not necessarily a narrative about wanting to be the other gender?

I'd like to end with a brief comment about a third kind of body modification television show—the trans-species narrative. While several of the "Humanimals" do not claim a trans-species identity—or any particular connection to the creatures they seek to resemble—an exception is a person the documentary refers to as Cat Man, or Dennis Avner. Cat Man has had forehead implants, his nose flattened, his cheeks filled with silicone, his top lip split, his teeth pulled and replaced with fangs, and whisker implants. He explains why he has chosen to modify himself to resemble a cat: "I do relate to my cats on an emotional level, an empathic level . . . I relate to cats on an entirely different level than most people . . . I react like a cat does, I see things as a cat does . . . it affects every aspect about me."[7]

This documentary also reaches into the past of its subjects, creating a narrative out of their childhood experiences, indeed even pathologizing their desire for extreme body modifications by emphasizing their divorced parents and experiences with abuse alongside their physical transformation and—particularly—their identification with non-human species. Cat Man's father abandoned his family, his mother remarried, his stepfather beat the children. The narrator speculates, "Perhaps the people who choose transformation are looking for a way to separate themselves from others." In an attempt to understand what produced the cat-like interior self, and the desire to make the physical human body conform to it, the narrative creates a pathologized inner being who, it argues, is seeking the ultimate form of social isolation. Cat Man is part Native American, and he cites this as one of the reasons behind his transformation. One question this raises is whether trans-species, in this case, can be thought of as a figure for race? Is this an attempt to achieve inclusion that will always be incomplete—particularly so, it might be argued, for Native Americans? Gender is not overtly a part of this narrative—but the narrative is similar to gender narratives in the way that it marks a disjunction between the inner self and the body. It is similar also because it records an effort to recover the self by trying to achieve—if incrementally— a kind of radical otherness. In the case of Cat Man, this radical otherness is even more interesting because it does not depend upon the regime of gender. As a viewer, I am left wondering what Cat Man can teach us about the possibility and the problematics of imagining, incorporating, and inhabiting that kind of radical otherness.

Notes

1. *The Swan* (Galan Entertainment/George Paige Associates Inc./A. Smith & Co./Freemantle Media, 2004).

2. Jay Prosser, *Second Skins: The Body Narratives of Transsexuality* (New York: Columbia University Press, 1998), p. 5.

3. Prosser, p. 65.

4. Changing Sexes: Female to Male (Discovery Communications, Inc., 2003).

5. Loren Cameron, *Body Alchemy: Transsexual Portraits* (Pittsburgh: Cleis Press, 1996); Ambroise Paré, *On Monsters and Marvels (Des monstres et prodiges)*, trans. Janis L. Pallister (Chicago: The University of Chicago Press, 1982), p. 33. Michel de Montaigne, in his *Essais*, discusses the story of Marie Germain, who transformed from a woman to a man while jumping over a stream; Ambroise Paré uses that story as an example as well.

6. Changing Sexes: Male to Female (Discovery Communications, Inc., 2003).

7. *Humanimals: Wild Makeovers* (Discovery Communications, Inc., 2003).

8

Interview

Aleshia Brevard with *Mary Weaver*

Aleshia Brevard: When I received an invitation to be on today's panel I was bewildered. I couldn't imagine why I'd been asked. I even tried to back out on several occasions. Then it finally sank in that this conference was being called "Bodies in the Making," and instantly I understood! Since George Jorgenson stepped off of a Danish operating table as Christine in 1952, transsexuals have indeed been bodies in the making. By some estimates there are 25,000 of us today. Let me stress that only a very few, a minuscule number, have ever appeared on the *Jerry Springer Show*.

At the time of my gender reassignment surgery in Los Angeles in 1962, I thought that would be enough body modification to last me for a lifetime. I wasn't counting, however, on Hollywood's fascination with the female bosom. You see, growing up labeled with the wrong gender hadn't caused enough traumas in my young life; I had to compound that by also wanting to be an actress. And after reassignment surgery acting might not have presented such a huge problem, had it not been for the popularity in the 1960s and 1970s of the sheer, see-through blouse. Female pulchritude, it turned out, carried more weight than did talent, when it came to landing an audition in Hollywood. So after graduate school a girlfriend and her husband financed my breast augmentation. That was my graduation gift. Very thoughtful, they were! The augmentation worked and, consequently, so did I. "Tits and Ass" was more than a popular song from the Broadway musical *A Chorus Line*.

All would have gone well in Hollywood if I could have remained in my twenties. So, I did my best to give the illusion that time was standing still—nothing major, you understand— just a little lid lift here and a little collagen there. And as I understand it that must be what qualifies me to be on today's panel.

Mary Weaver: Do you see many similarities or differences between your SRS (sexual reassignment surgery) and the other nips and tucks you've had during your career?

AB: Well, there are no similarities that I can see. By the way, the term "sexual reassignment surgery " just drives me crazy!

MW: What's your preferred term?

AB: Gender, I think. Gender reassignment. It has nothing to do with sex as far as I'm concerned—well, maybe on a good day.

To my way of thinking, the reassignment surgery was a lifesaving procedure. It was a surgery to correct an embarrassing, often threatening, birth defect. Beyond that, any further nips and tucks were for pure vanity, and/or a way to continue working in film and television for as long as possible.

MW: How might these similarities or differences relate to your thinking about being a woman in contemporary US society?

AB: I'm certainly not going to suggest that a nip here and a tuck there are going to make a woman any more legitimate or desirable. But as with everything else, I do believe that the choice for cosmetic surgery must reside with the woman. If having that nip or tuck is going to make her feel better about herself, if she can afford it, or even if she can't, it's still her choice to make.

I think a story that I want to share which might clarify how I feel about this. Several weeks ago I heard from a woman with whom I had done several films "back in the day." I had not heard from this old friend for over thirty years, and she tracked me down through a writer who was doing a retrospective on films done by Al Adamson. These were films that my friend and I had done together. Now this is a totally straight, traditionally heterosexual woman who's never had a gender crisis in her life, and was not aware of mine until the writer told her I had written a book. Do you know the first question she asked me, after over thirty years, and having just learned that her old acting crony was a transsexual? She said, "So tell me, Aleshia, how much work have you had done?" Later on, as an actress ages—it just sort of seems expected—"Did you get up this morning? Did you have plastic surgery?" After she told me about her own nips and tucks, she said, "You know when you were once a great beauty, that's a hard thing to turn loose of." And I guess for me that statement says all there is to say about an advertising-driven society where nothing less than pre-thirty-year-old perfection is allowed.

MW: How do you weigh the distinction between hormones and surgeries in light of building a body you're happy with? Which changes meant more, and which might you live without, if any?

AB: It was that initial gender corrective surgery that allowed me to live a happy, fulfilling life. Prior to that first surgery, I think it is true that the turmoil of my existence, the confusion with which I lived, impeded all personal and professional growth. So, it was that first surgery that was the all-important thing. The hormone treatment was merely a part of that package, although I will admit that the rounding of the body and the development of a bosom was a welcomed side effect. A couple of years after surgery I stopped taking hormones, because they made me too emotional, and I didn't take hormones for over forty years. I have only recently started again taking a low dose of Premarin, and that's basically for skin elasticity.

MW: But your initial dosage was really high compared to what you use now, right?

AB: I was sticking that stuff wherever I could find a place to stick it.

MW: You've mentioned the idea of living in stealth before. I was wondering if you could elaborate a bit on it.

AB: Well stealth, in case you don't know, is living under a rock, and I lived under that rock for almost forty years. I see some blank faces. . . . What I mean is, stealth is not acknowledging your transsexual being. It's just going about your life as though you were born in the gender that you have assumed. So it is in essence living under a rock, because you're not acknowledging your past. And I lived under that rock for almost forty years. Now during that time I was married four times, I raised three stepchildren, I had a career, which included eight films, thirty-six TV shows, and years of doing theater tours. I also did stints as a Playboy bunny, a showgirl, and ended up teaching theater in a university—East Tennessee University. And all the while living in stealth, living under my rock, terrified that my history was going to reach out and grab me by the throat. That's my stealth experience.

MW: You used to deflect certain questions; how did you do that?

AB: On first dates I would bring out pictures of "my four-year-old son." The picture was of a girlfriend's son, but I told my date—with tears—how my child . . . how this horrible man, who was the father of my child, had taken him fishing, didn't pay attention, and let my child drown. Now this is a horrible way to get around things, of course. Just killing off that kid off . . . whenever the need arose.

But the point is, once you do this, the man you're dating is not going to look up at a distraught mother and ask, "Could you have ever been raised as a male?"

MW: So what changed the living in stealth for you? What was the moment where you decided not to?

AB: An epiphany. I finally realized that to deny your history is to deny yourself.

MW: How do you feel in this post-living-in-stealth moment in terms of having a history that is just a bit more open? How has this changed interactions with people for the better or the worst?

AB: For me it's better. I do want to add, however, that I'm retired, so I'm no longer trying to work as an actress, or a Playboy bunny, or to teach at a Southern university. For an "out" transsexual there are just some clubs that you aren't invited to join. More importantly, clubs that just aren't going to hire you. So, I'm now retired; I work at writing. And even there I'm generally not labeled as a writer, but rather as "a transsexual writer". As I said to someone in the audience today, I'm sure when I pass over, it's going to read on my tombstone, "A transsexual lies here."

MW: When did you have your first cosmetic surgery, and are you planning on having more?

AB: Well, if we're calling it cosmetic, and supposedly we are, then the first surgery was the corrective surgery. That was in 1962. That was followed in about 1975 by the breast augmentation, and then maybe ten years after that we did this little lid lift. At the risk of sounding like a creation from Dr. Frankenstein's lab, I'm going to freely admit that I will be pumping up any little lines and indentations as long as they're pump-able.

MW: How do you relate your various cosmetic surgeries (and I'm actually not talking about your gender reassignment surgery) to your thinking on femininity?

AB: I don't see any relation at all. SRS did not make me a woman. It merely opened the door for me to be accepted as one.

MW: What about the other surgeries?

AB: Well, same thing, actually. They were for public presentation. I do think that we are living in a society where you are judged by what people first see. My experience has been that a fresher, more youthful appearance finds more acceptance. I think that's unfortunate, but I'm not making the rules, honey; I'm just trying to get through life as best I can.

MW: This is our last question. I know you're somewhat familiar with contemporary transgender and transsexual movements in the US. And I was wondering what you make of transpeople who opt not to have surgery, and or not to have hormones, and do you think this might relate to any changes in surgical techniques since your own corrective surgery?

AB: Well, this is a subject where I realize I can just go down in flames. But it is a subject on which my thinking has changed over the years. As one of the maiden transsexuals, a patient of Dr. Harry Benjamin, the doctor who coined the word "transsexual," I knew what his guidelines were. I adhered to those guidelines, rigidly. And, I will admit, I felt for many years that to be transsexual meant one must be exactly like me. I accepted, since the early guidelines were so narrow, that if you were not too pretty to survive as a male then you probably weren't transsexual. Now I have matured, I'm happy to say. I now realize that transsexuality is more than the curve of the ankle; it is a matter of heart and soul. It's what is on the inside. I cannot judge another's insides. So I think, as with everything else, how to express gender is the choice of the individual. I certainly applaud those who say, "I am just fine the way I was created." That simply wasn't true for me. I had to match what was on the inside with what was on the outside, and that included the whole works, the "nitty-gritty." Without a vagina I didn't feel I was complete, but I'm not going to make that an across the board judgment for everyone else.

Now, what do I make of transpeople who opt not to have surgery? Well, I'm still from the old school. Seems to me that the objective in life is to get through it with as much happiness as you can grab in both hands. For me happiness meant passing undetected through some very dark alleyways, home to those who wished me harm. And I do think that perhaps today my younger brothers and sisters are fighting for ways to illuminate the same dark places I found so threatening and so frightening. I wish them luck.

9

The Santa Cruz Tattoo Project

Kelley Richardson

Sometime around 1995, I am pulling into the parking lot of a restaurant out in Capitola. Parked across the lot from me is this big old 1965 Lincoln Continental in flat black primer, lowered, with suicide doors. That car has always been one of my personal favorites: a little bit muscle car and a little bit Addams Family. Just as I notice the customized chrome license plate frame, which reads "We are not our bodies," a woman

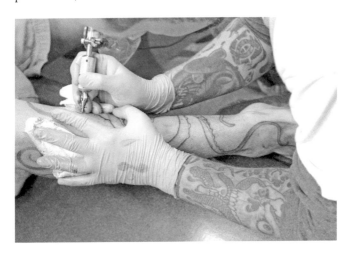

gets out of the car. She has long raven-black hair flowing all over, she is dressed all in black, wearing bright red lipstick, and she is *striking*. Her body is enormous, weighing probably 300 pounds. I just sit there in my car, in my skinny little body, in complete awe of this woman, and think to myself "Wow!" What an incredible statement.

I had never experienced someone so far outside my idea (at the time) of conventional beauty, who looked so great, who carried herself as confidently as this woman did, and who made such an intense impact that said simply "I am more than what you see." She was the extreme opposite of what I was trying to look like then, and yet she was so beautiful. The statement on that woman's license plate frame, "We are not our bodies," has haunted me and has helped form my understanding of the relationships that we share with our physical selves.

I have spent the past three years meeting, interacting with, and photographing hundreds of tattooed people in the community of Santa Cruz, California. I am intrigued by this unique genre of art and by the different people who have such artwork on their skin. This form of body modification has clearly moved beyond the conventional stereotype of the "tattooed

person." I have photographed doctors, lawyers, construction workers, airline pilots, students, teachers, tailors, psychiatrists, plumbers, professors, homeless people, former inmates, hair stylists, and people from countless other professions. They come from all walks of life, all socioeconomic backgrounds, and all levels of education.

Many of these people have come to my studio to have their portraits taken. Others I have met and photographed in the tattoo shops in town and out in the community: where they work, in their homes, at play. I have engaged in countless conversations about the artwork on people's bodies and why they have it. Generally speaking, most people were delighted to talk about their tattoos, but most of the conversations did not extend beyond the significance of the artwork itself. For example, some people explained that their tattoos, memorialize an event, a person, a relationship, a death, or a period in their life. But, save a small few, most conversations never developed to the next level of introspection to answer the deeper question: what causes you to want to inscribe your body with ink?

Being tattooed myself, the best I can do is to answer that question in my own words:

I am not this body I was born into
I was poured like potion in to some vessel,
    not of my own design,
Here I am trapped
Here is where I struggle
I want power and control
I want the right to design or redesign this thing
    that is my dwelling for a lifetime
This shaped has formed me
I have been forced to listen to the world calling me:
    what they see
And yet, it is not me, I am the inside
I am what you cannot see
And this struggle is my suffering
So I change it
I mark it
I scream out with who I actually am on the inside
I want it on the outside
I want to look in the mirror and see what I have made
Some days I want to show those marks to the world
    and make them wonder
When they start to think they might see who I am
I want to tell them, without words,
    that they don't know me
Some other days it will be my secret
    and only I will know what I have made
That I have transcended this flesh
I have navigated beyond these instructions
I have taken my psyche and mapped it on my skin

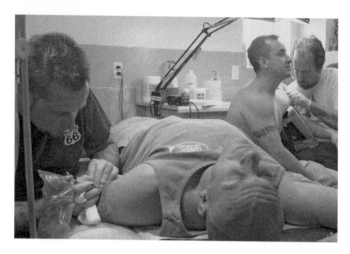

Writing these words, I revisited my lifelong pain caused by living with the body that I did not want but learned to tolerate. I think it is fantastic that today there is such a variety of ways that we can use to form our bodies into something of our own design: through decoration, surgery, or any of the many other types of body modifications. My pictures best relate my experiences with the people who have been so generous in sharing themselves with me. The images are meant to describe the identities that they revealed to me and my camera.

III
Inside/Outside

10

Embodiments and Disembodiments: The Relation of Body Modifications to Two Psychoanalytic Treatments

Sheila Namir

The tough-looking, monosyllabic, leather-clad tomboy street kid entered my consulting room resentfully. Everything about her a muscular second skin[1] except the doe-like eyes, soft as an infant's. From those first moments, my body became her projective object as I began experiencing her lack of embodiment in my body (as I embodied her disembodiment in my body)—containing and holding her inside myself from the beginning. There would be many sessions of silence; many weekends in which she wandered in a dissociated state and I would not leave my house for fear that she would feel "dropped" from my bodymind holding her. There were also many creative hours spent drawing or walking instead of talking despite the "talking cure" dictate. For months, I experienced "primary maternal preoccupation," that early sensitivity and adaptation of a mother to the survival and needs of her infant. Alienated from her abused body, she experienced her body only when cutting it. Feeling cut off from her affective and sensual aliveness, cutting her skin gave her both. Reclaiming her body from its deadness threatened to kill her.

Some years later, after she had found her voice to tell the story of her abuse, she showed me a tattoo—a baby bird falling from a nest with an arrow through it that she had used to represent what she couldn't say. Now she wanted it removed. And for the next months, this emblem and its fading became a symbol of what she no longer needed.

The other subject of this paper is a woman who hid in an entirely different way. I'd accuse her of "body deafness," of having "body agnosia." This Beverly Hills–looking American "man's woman" hid behind her desirable classical WASP mannequin self. Performing an "ideal femininity," her gender sculpting was an often conscious masquerade[2] to avoid her deeper or less socially agreeable feelings from being seen or known. Her made-up, constructed features and carefully adorned body were like invisibility cloaks, hiding her intelligence, psychic complexity and insecurities. Controlling how she was seen or not seen, she crafted her material presentation in an attempt to know what others gazed upon and to evacuate affect into the other. Her lack of bodily aliveness often communicated itself to me from behind the couch as a failure to receive or experience my rambunctious energy in her bodymind. I often felt my words and affect, my self, falling heavily at her feet like a dead tennis ball. Her compartmentalization of interior and exterior, and her rigidity and lack of fluidity were often what I sensed in her physical presence.

Her decision to have herself cut by having a face lift tore open the psychic envelope of my analysis, concretizing the space of the transitional, the transformative. Her decision to continue hiding in homogenization, looking as the world deemed attractive rather than emerging from her own aliveness, radiance, sensuality and self-expression, foreclosed a creative potential space for me.

As both analyst and analysand, I brought my own body-mind to these encounters. Different from both, in my hiding and in my revealing, psychic reality is shaped for me by embodied intersubjectivity. As an analyst who works from my bodily countertransference, I trust "knowing" myself and others through this pre-reflective embodiment. Sensitive to touch, smells, sounds and visceral sensations, I "know" in my bodily registers experiences that I cannot give names to and that often remain secret, silent and self-contained. Familiar with dissociative states, both how my body dissociates from my mind and my mind from my feelings, I rely strongly on this other "knowing" as a somatic, empathic immersion and recognition of the bodymind of another.

In this paper I am exploring the effects that body modifications have on the relational matrix in the culture of psychoanalytic treatment. Despite the fact that the "mind" is usually emphasized in psychoanalysis and the concrete "body" ignored, I want to assert that the body, as well as the psyche, is in process during therapy and that the intersubjective context and relationship are affected by these processes. The lived body in the context of the consulting room is the body I am discussing. The process between two communicative bodies is registered internally and externally in both, as each shapes and recognizes the other in a dialectical dance of sensations, sounds, movements, words, and resonances. The psychic space is a transitional one—neither inside nor outside—a creative area of experiencing. In this space, as in embodied experience, the "mind is extant throughout the body."[3] The plasticity of the mind and body to the social and emotional surround, both in construction and destruction, and the relational aspects of the bodymind are germane to this discussion. In my two clinical illustrations, when the skin as surface of the body becomes the focus, a concrete barrier is erected between the fluidity of psyche/soma, self/other, and inside/outside. This barrier impedes the imaginative work of psychoanalysis.

My thinking about the relational effects of body modifications during psychoanalytic treatment is based on my understanding of an infant's earliest experience of self and body through the body of another in its holding and handling of the infant.[4] If all goes well enough with the caregiver's holding, handling and personalization of the infant, psyche and soma are integrated. Without this "good enough" early experience, body and mind or soma and psyche split, and the achievement of becoming a person in a body who is related to others and the world is compromised.

The people I work with have less than optimal experiences of embodiment. The internal and external wounds, the injuries of sexuality, the early failures in "psychosomatic indwelling" because of impingements, intrusions and trauma are all registered in the bodymind. Depersonalization, dissociation, disintegration, and derealization are names that are given to the splits between mind and body and failures in embodiment in the psychoanalytic literature.

The forming of psychosomatic wholeness is obviously relational: the earliest experiences of the self in one's body are through the body of another. Our experiences of our bodies are in relation to other bodies from the beginning. We abandon or inhabit ourselves through the interactions with physical and psychological others. Bodies are known through other bodies, and body modifications affect other bodyminds, particularly in the close relations of analyst and analysand. Constituting each other, we practice bodymind communication in the therapeutic setting. When there are disembodied states, the communication is disabled or disaffected. When feelings are transcribed to the surface of the body for expression and possible transformation, there is the risk of abandoning the inside for the outside, of losing the complexity of mind and body to a dualistic reduction. Engaging, collapsing and affecting each other, the bodyminds of two subjects reproduce self and other, interior and exterior, in surfaces and depths of multidimensional space and time.

Returning to the consulting room with my patient—her body seems tense, she stares at me with hard eyes, struggling wordlessly to tell me what she is experiencing. Self-cutting has been her language of aliveness and her self-cure for feelings of deadness. The blood proves to her she has an inside to which she has access while others don't. The self-infliction and the mastery of pain reassure her that she doesn't need others, can heal herself. Most of all, the self-cutting obliterates the memory of her rape at age fourteen. Her scars are external, not internal; self not other-imposed. "I need to cut," she says, "I need to feel the blood" as her palm is held in front of her, between us. "I want the blood to flow into my hand." I was not watching her body, was not witness to her outstretched hand, but was anticipating and feeling the cut and the blood down my arm. Without thinking, in a moment of feeling what the warm blood would feel like in her palm, I placed my palm on hers. She looked at me startled, tears filling her eyes, and her body relaxed.

The next session, she walked in and handed me her cutting knife, saying "I can't cut now—it would be like cutting you." Sometime later, I understood more about her need for my body to experience what she was cut off from; her need for me to contain and express her body in mine. One very silent session, with L. twirling on the chair and looking away from me, I felt protoplasmic pulsation in my body as though I was expanding. I experienced myself growing larger, softer, amoeba-like round and I remember thinking that perhaps I had become a large lap that my patient wanted to sit in. I let the sensations continue without moving. My patient got off the chair, lay down on the couch and began telling me, for the first time, the story of her sexual abuse. Somehow I had communicated that I could hold her, that my body was soft and not dangerous, that she could safely sink into it as a couch.

The meanings and practices of bodies affecting each other is an important aspect of psychoanalytic work. Not the body as an object in which to read pathology or a mind that is developed to control the body. Rather, these are bodyminds developing and continuing a process of dialectical communication and dialogue in the intersubjective world and transitional space of psychoanalysis. The meanings of these bodies and minds are the work of psychotherapy and psychoanalysis—meaning-making in consort with other bodies.

As a witness to my patient's tattoo removal I was able to help her to attend to her body in a way she hadn't before. Just as tattooing can expand the sense of self-identity and embodiment, the removal of a tattoo can serve the same purpose. Reclamation of her body was paradoxically achieved by this "unwriting" of the body, which gave her more fluidity and a more open embodiment. This was also a time of shared pain—what she had experienced earlier in her life as silent and traumatic pain had now been told and the healing of her lasered skin was a reflection of her internal healing.

Writing on the body is one way of expressing to oneself and to others many aspects of the presentation, performance, politics, principles and practices of self. As an affective mnemonic, as one person called it,[5] tattoos may memorialize events, states, relationships and affects. Altering one's face and body may be ways of shaping one's psychic and affective being, of opening or of foreclosing possibilities. I'm not arguing here for the meanings of body modification in a theoretical or political or even in a particularly feminist way. I am arguing rather for the intersubjective meaning of these modifications in two analytic treatments. At the heart of therapy is the exploration and expression of internal worlds in relation to another. When that exploration and expression are concretized rather than elaborated in an imaginative realm, then the self is experienced as "one-bodied" rather than "two-or-more-bodied," and the intersubjective domain remains unrecognized or foreclosed.

My analyst's decision to have cosmetic surgery was difficult for me to experience as her act of empowerment or self-determination within the context of our dyadic world. Although she was not a particularly politically principled person or a feminist in her consciousness, we had still been able to create a space for deep reflective engagement and exploration. The primacy of our internal worlds and a shared conviction that change occurred in that realm were germane to our work. Her sudden focus on the facticity of the body, of her face, concretized the shimmering elasticity of the imaginary body created for holding in a transitional, transformative space. The bodymind that lived within the analytic experience became sharply demarcated into body, face, mind and products that were socially and culturally dictated. To see her face as an object for repair, as a construction and commodity given over to a surgeon, threatened the creative process of seeing and being seen in fluid apperception. I feared the fixed and unresponsive face,[6] the feeling of unreality it elicited in my bodymind history. The closed systems of dissociated body and mind, self and other, internal and external worlds, were early solutions to my own traumatic history and somatic memories.

Her body as surface belied the complexity of bodymind. It also belied the potential for embodiment in the analytic holding and handling of the relationship I felt necessary for my own work. Instead, I felt forced, in our bodymind, in the psychic envelope of the dyadic relation, to experience her wounding and cutting. Her surgery also focused me on the visual. I wanted to see the results of her cutting, and the stitches, the swelling, and the palette of colors were painful to my eyes and to my psyche. Attachment, containment and relatedness were all affected by her decision to address her insecurities and fears in this concrete manner. I was transported from the depths of internal work to the surface of the sociocultural world in a painful and premature expulsion from a psychic womb.

With my patient, I was able, through my embodied experience and my recognition of her, to help her to narrate her pain and suffering and to eventually become embodied. Her need to dissociate from her pain by cutting and marking her body, and her avoidance of her sexual body and desire for other bodies, gradually changed during her analysis. I am convinced that if I practiced psychotherapy and psychoanalysis in a culture of mind rather than in one of bodymind, I would not have been affected by her body modifications and I would not have been able to help her find their meanings for herself.

Psychoanalysis is a *praxis* of the body, mind and affects through embodiment. Attempting to create, recognize and communicate the complexity of bodyminds in all of their permutations and expressions is how I understand the work. So, in my own analysis, I lost the possibility for communicative embodiment when my analyst opted for cosmetic surgery. I had to face the fact that I couldn't create the meanings I needed with her and it was the beginning of the end of our work. She could not share my personal and professional struggle to embrace the importance of embodiment and to live from that place in the analytic space. In fact, she could not be the bodymind I needed and the effect of her body modification was to create a wound that we could not heal and a split that she could not help me to bridge.

Training in psychoanalysis, both theoretically and clinically, focuses on the mind: theories of the mind, development of the mind, understanding the conscious and unconscious mind. The space that has tended to be overlooked in psychoanalysis is the transcendence of the mind-body split and its centrality for both patient and analyst. I learned through my experience as an analyst with this patient and other patients the effectiveness of working through the embodied presence of both—although the "embodied analyst" was not deemed an achievement in my training. I also learned that the disembodied analyst cannot find the embodied other nor can she help another to experience embodiment. Body modifications, body projects, like everything else in life, achieve their meanings in the intersubjective world. Our bodies are made in relation to other bodies, and body modifications affect these relations, as I have tried to illustrate through examples of crucial bodymind interactions in two analytic dyads. This perspective has significant implications for psychoanalytic theory as well as for clinical practice.

Notes

1. Esther Bick, "The Experience of Skin in Early Object Relations," *International Journal of Psychoanalysis* 49 (1968), pp. 484–486.

2. Joan Riviere, "Womanliness as a Masquerade," *International Journal of Psychoanalysis* 9 (1929), pp. 303–313.

3. Eugenio Gaddini, "Notes on the Mind-Body Question," In *A Psychoanalytic Theory of Infantile Experience: Conceptual and Clinical Reflections.* (London and New York: Tavistock/Routledge, 1992), p. 120.

4. Eugenio Gaddini, *ibid.,* pp. 119–141. Donald W. Winnicott, "Mind and Its Relation to the Psyche-Soma,"(1949) in *Through Paediatrics to Psychoanalysis* (New York: Basic Books, 1975). Donald W. Winnicott, "The Theory of the Parent-Infant Relationship." (1960) in *The Maturational Process and the Facilitating Environment: Studies in the Theory of Emotional Development* (New York: International Universities Press, Inc., 1965). Donald W. Winnicott, "Mirror-Role of Mother and Family in Child Development" (1967) in *Playing and Reality* (London and New York: Routledge, 1971).

5. Jody Greene, personal communication to the author, July 27, 2005.

6. Donald W. Winnicott, *ibid.,* 1967.

11

Cutting Through Race and Class: Women of Color and Self-Injury

Gabriela Sandoval

Cutting one's body, cutting the skin on one's own arms and legs, for example, is the most prevalent form of episodic, superficial/moderate, self-injurious behavior. Self-injury is deliberate: it involves the destruction of body tissue without the intent to kill oneself. In their studies, mental health professionals have constructed self-cutting as a problem affecting privileged, educated, young, middle-class, white women (some authors go so far as to add "attractive" to the list of descriptors). Self-injury is also widely understood to be a *symptom* of other disorders as opposed to standing alone. Thus, the young, white, privileged self-injurer populating the mental health professional's imagination often manifests self-injurious behavior as a symptom of personality, post-traumatic stress, eating and dissociative disorders. Portrayals of self-injury in the popular media have also served to embed this version of the stereotypical "cutter" in the public psyche.

In this paper, I argue that self-injurious behavior among non-stereotypical "cutters" has something important to tell us about the way race, class, gender and sexuality intersect.

However, mine is *not* a "multicultural" endeavor. I am not simply attempting to tack on, if you will, the voices of women of color who have been left out of samples that privilege the voices of young, white, middle-class women. Rather, I am looking at these acts of self-injury as coping mechanisms and asking what they can tell us about immigration, cultural dissonance, sexuality and class mobility—as these are made tangible at the moment when body tissue is destroyed.

During the 2000–2001 academic year, I worked at an Ivy League university as the director of a residence hall that housed fifty-seven students, the vast majority of whom were students of color. During that time, I became aware that several of the residents in my hall self-injured. I had never been directly exposed to self-injury before, but I knew that the stereotypical self-injurer was white, middle-class, and female. Besides being female, however, these students did not fit the accepted labels: they were Latinas, from immigrant families. Their parents had worked their way out of the working class and tentatively into the ranks of the middle class. They were also the first generation of college students in their families. I became intrigued.

My first source for information on self-injury was the internet. There I found an abundance of material about the topic, everything from how best to be supportive of someone who self-injures to information for people who self-injure and are looking for strategies to resist being "helped." Much of the popular and, therefore, most of the accessible literature on cutting and other forms of self-injury, states emphatically that self-injury affects populations regardless of class, gender, and race. Nevertheless, most of what is known about self-injury is documented in mental health literature based on data from small samples that are overwhelmingly female, middle- and upper-middle-class, well-educated, young and white. Furthermore, the meanings attached to self-injurious behavior among women of color are problematically racialized. Such behavior is most often seen as an expression of feelings of anger and is not understood as a coping mechanism and a valid form of psychological release.

What struck me about the students and their understanding of their self-injurious behavior had to do with the social context within which it took place. These young women often rehearsed a very specific narrative about themselves and their families—not always in the context of self-injury. They saw themselves as incredibly fortunate to be at such a prestigious university and, during our conversations about their feelings, they often expressed gratitude toward their parents for the sacrifices they had made as immigrants and for enabling their children's social mobility. They also regularly dismissed their own difficulties with academic and social pressures, especially when they contrasted those difficulties with the obstacles their parents had overcome in order to provide educational opportunities for them. They argued that they could not complain about their difficulties, their fears, or the obstacles they encountered because these simply did not compare to the challenges their parents had faced in leaving their home countries, their families, and their jobs in order to come to cities in the United States where they felt unwelcome, did not speak the language, and were not familiar with the culture.

In most ways, the cutting I was made aware of among these Latina students (usually by my staff of residence advisors) was very similar to that which has been documented in the mental health literature. They were not attempting suicide. They were secretive about their cutting. And since living in such close proximity to one another made it difficult to keep their actions and/or scars hidden from roommates, their roommates were usually the first at school to realize that they were self-injuring. They also usually felt a need to cut in an effort to feel alive and they used it as a strategy for coping with psychic distress.

For these students, then, cutting was a coping mechanism, which served a specific and complex purpose. It was an expression of their feelings about the disparity between their own and their parents' experience and, because of the form it took, it both violated and maintained the silence that they and their families had preserved around these issues of difference.

Agreeing with Natasha Alexander and Linda Clare's study of self-injury among women with lesbian and bisexual identities (2004), I want to argue that self-injury arises, "not as a symptom of individual intra-psychic disorder, but as a coping response that arises within a social context".[1] Further, I want to extend the argument of Sarah Naomi Shaw (2002) that self-injury "reflects girls' and women's experiences of relational and cultural violations, silencing and objectification."[2] I would add that class—and class mobility—intersect with race to create unique circumstances in which women of color use self-injury as a way to reconcile class disjunctures or disjunctures between their own racial identities and those of their parents. Additionally, I want to argue that self-injurious behavior is an understandable response not only to patriarchal and heterosexist cultural norms, but also to stereotypical norms of race and class. Thus, self-injurious acts undertaken by working-class (or formerly working-class) women of color—among whom class and race intersect to create unique, and as yet unexplored, circumstances—can be understood as efforts to reconcile disjuncture and dissonance among their class and racial identities. The inclusion of women of color and queer women in the current discourse of cutting requires that we take into account racist, classed and heterosexist—as well as patriarchal—structures of society and the pressures they exert as the imagined pristine smoothness of brown skin is disrupted by the cutting implement.

Notes

1. Natasha Alexander and Linda Clare, "You Still Feel Different: The Experience and Meaning of Women's Self-injury in the Context of a Lesbian or Bisexual Identity," *Journal of Community & Applied Social Psychiatry* 14 (1998), p. 83.

2. Sarah Naomi Shaw, "Shifting Conversations on Girls' and Women's Self-Injury: An Analysis of the Clinical Literature in Historical Context," *Feminism & Psychology* 12 (2002), p. 192.

12

Borderlines In and Out of Prison

Lorna A. Rhodes

How do we know that understanding (the finding of "intelligible relations") is a function of the patient rather than of something in the explainer—his zeal, the elasticity of his interpretive concepts, his empathic skills, or perhaps his ability to find schizoid elements within himself?
—Louis A. Sass,
Madness and Modernism:
Insanity in the Light of Modern Art,
Literature and Thought
(New York: Basic Books, 1992), p. 26

This paper had its starting point early in my work on prisons. Eventually I and my colleagues at the University of Washington studied the state's supermaximum prisons, where I conducted ethnographic research and where we interviewed almost a hundred prisoners in lockdown.[1] But when we first began to work with the state Department of Corrections, the facility most open to us was a prison psychiatric treatment unit that I will call here "Mental Health Unit" or MHU, where severely mentally ill prisoners were treated with medication and behavioral therapy. Although also a lockdown facility, it had greater numbers of mental health staff and a more flexible regime than other lockdown units in the state.

The US prison complex forms a fraught, uneven boundary with institutional psychiatry, and MHU sat squarely at this border.[2] Here I consider one sort of event that occurred at this prison: some prisoners, usually diagnosed as "borderlines," cut, mutilate and otherwise harmed themselves. These prisoners were few in number in the context of the prison complex as a whole; Washington State alone has some 17,000 prisoners. But in this small, all-male unit intended for the system's mentally ill inmates, self-harm was a frequent occurrence. It was a medical emergency that required immediate intervention by clinical staff and that set in motion a chain of bureaucratic reactivity. It was also an expressive act whose meaning was over-determined and contested. Cutting, near-hanging, self-mutilation and swallowing sharp objects appear as bodily enactments of emotional pain that teeter at the brink of suicide. Prison staff, however, considered them an extreme and all too effective bid for attention.[3]

This essay proceeds through a series of associative leaps inspired in part by my own experience of the interior aesthetic and emotional atmosphere in maximum security prisons. Although the protagonist is a diagnostic category, I touch briefly at the end on my larger goal, which is to diagnose symptoms occurring elsewhere in the prison system as a whole and, ultimately, in the body politic.[4] Perhaps by considering routine emergencies in a small corner of a medium-sized state system, we can gain some small purchase on how a larger emergency unfolds, and is interpreted, at the level of the national penal complex.

Uncoupling and the Schizoid Position

> . . . I felt that everything was inevitably there, but for no reason and without any meaning . . .
>
> —Georgio de Chirico, quoted in Sass, *Madness and Modernism*, p. 44

Although prisons themselves are generally hidden from public view—in fact, increasingly so over the past thirty years of massive expansion—we are surrounded by fictional and media images of the prison environment. It is easy to take for granted some of its peculiar features and difficult to imagine that these constitute a living environment, a *home*, for two million people. Further, the "prison" of the nineteenth century, so central to academic theorizing about power and subjection, had qualities as a living space that are no longer present in contemporary prisons.[5] The interiors of nineteenth- and early twentieth-century institutions were relatively small, with dim lighting, labyrinthine hallways, chaotic cellblocks, and gates that required enormous keys. Some of these older prisons are still in use as general population (less-than-maximum-security) facilities, though increasingly they are being converted to museums.

Contemporary lockdown prisons, on the other hand, are characterized by intense, white, all-pervasive artificial light, uniform concrete and plastic surfaces, computerized operating systems, sophisticated surveillance, and large empty expanses, sometimes painted with bright colors. Cells have flat lighting panels illuminated around the clock, smooth featureless walls, shiny metal fixtures, and frosted or thick plastic windows encased in concrete and steel. In other words, while nineteenth-century prisons resembled the factories and workhouses of that era, these new facilities mirror the industrial aesthetic of the late twentieth century: they are big, bright, hard-edged, efficient warehouses. Film and television depictions of contemporary prisons capture this atmosphere to some extent, but they tend to exaggerate the size of cell interiors, the degree of privacy, and the amount of color and visual complexity.

MHU was characterized by a style we might call "early supermax." It was a lockdown environment—in which inmates are held in single cells under intensive surveillance—with most of the aesthetic qualities I've just described. But because it was a psychiatric facility, conditions for individual inmates varied somewhat; some were held in their cells almost around the clock, while others had some freedom to spend time together in day rooms and small yards.[6] Like a psychiatric hospital ward, MHU had small domestic flourishes. Murals were painted on the sides of unit control booths, an occasional plant graced a windowsill, and day rooms were sometimes used for homey projects like making Christmas ornaments.

Louis Sass draws a connection between modernist art and the inner perceptual and emotional world of schizophrenic patients. The paintings of de Chirico, for instance, depict space that is both flat and surreally expanded. Strange, dissociated objects float in an eerie, even light. The feeling is of "illuminated emptiness, strangeness, or devitalization . . . objects take on the look of 'stage accessories' . . . and people seem mere . . . 'automatons'" (48).[7] Sass points to striking similarities between this aesthetic and descriptions of the pre-psychotic or schizoid state that precedes a full psychotic break. This state involves, first, a sense of disconnection and "separation from the social and external world" in which experience is "dominated by [an] awareness of distance, difference and fragmentation" (90). Second, it involves what Sass refers to as "uncoupling." Uncoupling ". . . sets up a division between two different selves: a hidden, 'interior' self that watches or controls, usually associated with the mind, and a public, outer self that is more closely identified with bodily appearance and social role and that tends to be felt as somehow false or unreal" (97). Sass suggests both that this distanced, fragmented, self-monitoring schizoid state is specific to modernity, and that modernist art and literature make visible the inner contours of schizoid perception. He does not, however, extend his thesis to the environments patients generally live in today, nor to the modernist influence on the look and feel of contemporary institutional space.

But if we take Sass's argument in this direction, we might consider MHU a "disconnecting" and "uncoupling" environment. First, of course, it disconnected the prisoner from the outside world and inserted him into a devitalized and regimented institutional space. And second, it placed him in a panoptical and mechanical relation to himself, thus producing the "uncoupling" that, in Sass's formulation, constitutes the schizoid position on and in the world. The kind of behavior deemed "appropriate" to such a position might include indifference, automatic compliance, and muted emotional expression—the very qualities prisoners say they must cultivate to survive the settings in which they live.

Splitting Bodies/Feelings/Groups

> You're a problem because you are a problem,
> not because you have a problem.
>
> —Prison mental health worker

When I met one prisoner identified as a self-mutilator, an officer brought him to his long-term counselor's office, a small room fronted—for safety—by a large glass wall. The counselor asked him about what he had done to himself.

Prisoner: It's a behavior that works for me, I get some kind of release. The first time I was eighteen and in [a medium security prison]. I had never been in a mental hospital, I didn't know people cut themselves. I was so depressed, extremely depressed. I just took a razor blade and cut my arm, it didn't even hurt.

Mental health worker: When you reached for the razor blade did you know it was going to happen?

Prisoner: It was spontaneous. I just did it, I didn't know . . .

The first time, they took me to the infirmary and stitched me up and gave me counseling. . . . I was suffering inside, I was really angry inside. I didn't cut myself to commit suicide. I quickly learned the difference between a suicide gesture and a suicide attempt. I was saying, hey, I'm hurting, I'm in pain.

This man insisted on the fact of his suffering and on his possession of an "inside" where he was angry and hurting. But he had also learned the perspective of his caretakers on how a "gesture" develops into a "behavior" that "works." When his counselor asked whether he "knew he was going to do it," the question distinguished the moment of starting—in retrospect a kind of innocence—with the calculation regarded in this setting as inherent in attention-gaining acts.

The intense engagement of MHU staff with the diagnosis of borderline personality forms the backdrop of this conversation. The *Diagnostic and Statistical Manual of Mental Disorders (DSM)* distinguishes personality disorders from the major mental illnesses, meaning that they constitute "traits" or aspects of "character" rather than "states" of illness. Borderlines are described as having "affective instability," "impulsivity," and "chronic feelings of emptiness"; they engage in suicidal gestures, self-mutilation, and "frantic efforts to avoid real or imagined abandonment." Discussion of borderlines—in and beyond the prison context—centers on their emotional intensity and unpredictability, qualities said to cause those in contact with them to experience emotion as a problem for *themselves*. Because the borderline is characterized by "unstable . . . relationships with extremes of idealization and devaluation," he "splits" others by projecting this internal instability into them. The inmates' problem becomes a problem for his keepers not only because his behavior produces an uproar in the institutional environment, but because he provokes in those around him an extreme and bewildering emotional reactivity.[8]

Some 75% of those diagnosed with borderline personality disorder are women.[9] If MHU found itself with a "specialty" of borderline men, this may speak to the concentration of those men who do carry the diagnosis in prisons rather than hospitals. But the point I want to make here is that the diagnostic category (and, to a greater or lesser extent, the people in it[10]) represents an option both for expressing features of the prison environment—those modernist features that Sass suggests are parallel to psychic processes of dissociation—and for resisting these same features. It is the element of resistance that brings to bear the main tool of MHU clinical staff: the "behavior modification agreement" or BMA.

Emotion and Neutrality

> [Behaviorists] would be entirely neutral—they had no axes to grind, no prejudices to foist. They would be "neutralists" and "technicians" . . . so adept at engineering the situation of human beings that the engineered person would scarcely know it had happened.
>
> —Rebecca Lemov,
> *World as Laboratory:*
> *Experiments with Mice, Mazes and Men,*
> (New York: Hill and Wang, 2005,
> describing American behaviorism in the 1930s)

Prisoners in lockdown facilities live in a state of fairly minimal bodily existence; they lack independent access to basic amenities, are radically restricted in their actions, and have no control over others' access to their persons. Further, incarceration is usually numbingly boring. The emergency of self-harm disrupts this state—what we might call, following Agamben, "bare life" and, following Sass,[11] "the schizoid/modernist aesthetic"—with a demand for reaction. MHU staff attributes this to the inner condition of the inmate; borderlines, said one mental health worker, "Have no core feelings. They need you to feel for them." Although the emptiness of the maximum security environment—its quality of being drained of softness, feeling and unpredictability—does not figure explicitly in this explanation, this person went on to say "they like to create chaos so they're not bored. They get feelings out it. They want staff reaction—anger, liking."[12] It is this wanting, this desire, that constituted the primary resource for developing a behavioral modification approach for each inmate.

MHU staff developed BMAs at staff meetings intended both to harmonize the differing perspectives of treatment and custody staff and to pool staff knowledge of prisoners' lives.[13] "The inmate needs a carrot," explained one staff member, and the behavioral plan was a map for matching that carrot with the desired behavior. Staff, however, had few carrots to offer. One mental health worker said sadly, "I'm the old behaviorist who thought he could have a positive impact. I used to bring granola bars for the guys. But I've been defeated; I got in a lot of trouble." In the punitive atmosphere of contemporary corrections, the most practical way to "modify" behavior is to take something away. Thus in one meeting about a prisoner whose plan was being "band-aided all over the place," staff decided that his one motivator was smoking; they agreed to take away his smoke break so that they could give it back for good behavior.

In cases where the resistance expressed in cutting seemed particularly obvious to staff, the "solution" could be sharply punitive. One staff member explained how they had kept a prisoner's self-harm from "working" for him.

He is a Department of Corrections creation. He says, I've got problems, I'm gonna cut myself, I'm gonna hang myself. With all the political ramifications, here we go. We say, you're going to the hospital. He says, no, and threatens to cut. We have to call everyone but the Secretary—there's all this protocol. So we tell him if he threatens to cut we will use pepper spray. He hasn't done it in months.

Here "behavior modification" provides a vocabulary of studied neutrality that papers over frustration and anger with what was once called "human engineering" (148).[14] But this same neutrality also allows a more positive, instrumental deployment of the one "reinforcer" most readily available (and less visible than granola bars)—human interaction. As one mental health worker explained, "You put your attention on appropriate behavior and *tell* him how glad you are about it."

MHU staff thus saw their own reactivity—whether anger, disgust, compassion, or approval—as prisoners' primary motivator and believed that only through emotional self-management could they avoid reinforcing negative acts. One mental health worker described those prisoners who "swallow things [like] razor blades, safety pins, forks" and the response of her unit.

With swallowers, our reaction can prolong the episode. We used to send them to [the state hospital]—they would cut them open and take stuff out. [But] these guys are trying to get attention—the more you give the more they will do what you're trying to stop. So we came up with a protocol regarding the size of the object and let stuff pass.

Another described the same strategy of non-attention for cutting. "Now we use 4-pt. beds. We move the cutter to the infirmary and strap him down to restrain him from doing it. . . . They up ante to get attention and will do really bizarre things." Prisoners themselves did not speak about attention in this way unless prompted. When asked whether he acted for attention one man said, "I can't really associate to that, but I feel better after I see the skin break and the blood dribble down. I get a little release. There are other reasons: anger, hostility, confusion."

I have thus far brought together three things. First, the prison environment favors and mirrors a schizoid position—that is, a position of distance, objectification, and impersonality. Second, "borderline personality disorder" is psychiatric shorthand for people who seem to be enacting *both* numbness and intense emotion, and whose unpredictability disrupts the flat surface of normal operation.[15] And third, behavioral techniques reinforce the schizoid position of distancing and refusal to respond. When a "cutter" or "swallower" is tied down in front of a camera, "splitting" is happening on many dimensions: in the aesthetic qualities of the setting, in distancing of the staff, and in the "uncoupling" of self and observer. Whether or not it is happening inside the prisoner is open to question, since we might, at this point, suspect that he is serving as a screen for these complex projections.

There is a fourth split as well, not the one that happens when the inmate is being ignored, but the one deployed when his desire is met by the planned institutional reinforcement. When not interaction itself (commonly offered in tandem with the routines of feeding and hygiene), these rewards are often small bits of everyday life, of a piece with the "domestic" aspect of the institutional interior: being allowed to wear one's own clothes, to work in the kitchen, or to watch TV. Describing the success of a BMA, one prison worker described the taming of his behavior:

[That inmate] would whine, complain, make weapons. He was locked down most of the time. I walked in this morning and he's mopping the floor, dressed neatly. His management plan was real clear and he's taking advantage of it.

The "borderline," then, is the place where an emotional, acting-out prisoner with a "feminine" diagnosis is subject to—and helped to "want"—the few domestic, homey rewards the staff can offer, including their basic attention.[16] The inmate who splits open his body—as though mocking the panoptical principle of transparency while bloodying the shiny interiors that support it —is encouraged instead to join the staff in the seemingly neutral task of maintaining the clean surfaces of those same interiors. The resulting docility succeeds—at least temporarily—in bypassing the "imbroglio"[17] produced when the inherent contradictions of behaviorism meet the unstable emotions and identifications of the "borderline."

Conclusion

> . . . today's crime control strategies have a certain "fit" with the structures of late modern society . . . but such policies are not inevitable.
>
> —David Garland,
> *The Culture of Control:*
> *Crime and Social Order*
> *in Contemporary Society*
> (Chicago: University of Chicago Press, 2001), p. 201

The practice of some form of behavioral technology and the underlying premises I have described are widespread in prisons, particularly in supermax facilities. They deserve more attention than I have been able to offer here. But I want to conclude with a speculation that points to the "diagnosis" of a larger condition.

The past thirty years of penal expansion have given us a correspondingly expansive literature. The bulk of this production falls onto the two ends of a continuum. On the one hand, numerous trade journals, management tracts and how-to books are written by prison administrators and others invested in the system; on the other hand, there is an increasing proliferation of critiques "against" the prison complex by former prisoners, human rights advocates, journalists and others on the "outside." If one reads across these genres, one is struck by the concentration of dry, "neutral" language at one end and intense, feeling-full language at the other. I am painting with a very broad brush here, and there are many exceptions and complications (for example, academic critics tend to enlist prisoners to "feel for them" in their writing). But I am suggesting that it is as though the expression of emotion occurs in proportion to one's inability to effect any actual change "inside." Administrative policies, proposals and descriptions of systems and programs resemble "behavior management agreements" and tend to perpetuate the very depersonalization and schizoid environments that contribute to the problems they hope to resolve. At the same time, those who rage from the periphery are ignored as though they were "acting out." In other words, "splitting" does not only happen in specialized places housing people called borderlines—it also characterizes the border between the prison and the outside world. Perhaps we should take this, too, as the sign of an emergency, a symptom among many others of the untenable situation that is the US prison complex.

Notes

1. In 1993 the University of Washington and the Washington State Department of Corrections formed a legislatively supported collaborative relationship based in the School of Nursing and directed by David Allen. We worked with corrections staff on projects (such as, for example, helping establish a medium-security psychiatric unit) and eventually conducted research both on the state's supermax facilities and on mental health treatment across security levels. It is important to note, especially in the context of this article, that I worked entirely in all-male institutions. I thank everyone who has made my work possible, especially prisoners and staff at several institutions, David Lovell, David Allen, and my colleagues in the Department of Anthropology. I also thank Helene Moglen and Nancy Chen for providing the opportunity to present this piece at the "Bodies in the Making" conference. The focus on emotion in my argument here was sparked by a comment Emily Martin made about an earlier work, for which I thank her. I have changed institutional and personal details to protect confidentiality, written in the past tense to indicate that changes have occurred in this setting since the 1990s when the research was conducted, and edited quotes slightly for length and clarity.

2. I have written elsewhere about the relationship between supermax (maximum security lockdown) facilities and mental health treatment in prison, about the use of psychiatric diagnosis in the context of mass incarceration, and about the prison as an economy of attention. See Lorna A. Rhodes, "Taxonomic Anxieties: Axis I and II in Prison," *Medical Anthropology Quarterly* 14 (2000):346-73; "Psychopathy and

the Face of Control in Supermax," *Ethnography* 3 (2002): 445-69; *Total Confinement: Madness and Reason in the Maximum Security Prison* (Berkeley: University of California Press, 2004). See also, among many others, Michael Tonry and Joan Petersilia, eds., *Prisons* (Chicago: Chicago University Press, 1999) and David Garland, *The Culture of Control: Crime and Social Order in Contemporary Society* (Chicago: University of Chicago Press, 2001) on the political and social context of contemporary regimes of punishment.

3. Self-mutilation happens outside prison, of course, and has inspired a large popular and self-help literature with an overwhelming emphasis on teenage girls. I am treating it here only as it is specific to the prison context—men often start in prison—and am not making a psychological argument about its cause either in or outside prison.

4. Lorna A. Rhodes, "Panoptical Intimacies," *Public Culture* 10 (1998): 285-311; Lila Abu-Lughod, "The Romance of Resistance: Tracing Transformations of Power through Bedouin Women," *American Ethnologist* 17(1990): 41-55.

5. Cf. Michel Foucault, *Discipline and Punish: The Birth of the Prison* (New York: Vintage Press, 1979).

6. As a psychiatric facility, MHU is staffed with mental health as well as custody workers; the work of examination, record-keeping, medication and daily caretaking is similar to that of a public psychiatric hospital, but takes place alongside the work of counting, guarding, and punishing. Many of the inmates are severely mentally ill; "guilty by reason of insanity" convictions, which lead to psychiatric hospitalization, are rare in Washington State.

7. Louis A. Sass, *Madness and Modernism: Insanity in the Light of Modern Art, Literature and Thought* (New York: Basic Books, 1992) paraphrasing "Renee," the subject of M. Sechehaye's *Autobiography of a Schizophrenic Girl* (New York: New American Library, 1970). Sass uses de Chirico's 1914 "The Enigma of a Day" and de Chirico's writings about his own state of mind to introduce his thesis that certain mental states connect with the modernist sensibility. Sass takes his descriptive terms from his own patients and the writings of others diagnosed with schizophrenia. One of his examples is Daniel Paul Schreber, the nineteenth-century German patient whose writings influenced Freud's description of paranoid schizophrenia; Sass frames his own argument about Schreber in terms of the panoptical relation of subjection and self-monitoring.

8. *Diagnostic and Statistical Manual of Mental Disorders, Fourth Edition—Text Revision* (*DSM IV -- TR: 301.83*) (Washington D.C.: American Psychiatric Association, 2000). The *DSM* organizes disorders

along several "axes," most important of which are Axis I for the major mental disorders (that is, schizophrenia, bipolar disorder) and Axis II for the personality disorders. Borderline personality disorder is in Cluster B, the "dramatic, emotional and erratic" disorders, and has given rise to a large and confusing literature. Since the early 1990's, however, the work of Marsha M. Linehan (*Cognitive-Behavioral Treatment of Borderline Personality Disorder* (New York: Guilford Press, 1993) has exerted a clarifying influence on understanding and treatment of the disorder; Linehan does not accept the notion that borderlines are "manipulating" their therapists. In prison mental health facilities, where staff is overwhelmed with pressure on their beds from the acutely mentally ill, there is a certain simplification of issues surrounding the personality disorders.

9. *Diagnostic and Statistical Manual of Mental Disorders, Fourth Edition—Text Revision* (*DSM IV -- TR: 301.83*). Charles Nuckolls suggests in *Culture: A Problem That Cannot Be Solved* (Madison: University of Wisconsin Press, 1998) that the personality disorders as they are described in the psychiatric classification system (as Axis II in the DSM) are a symbolic representation that reflects specifically American enactments of gender. The emotional, histrionic, "manipulative" and attention-gaining disorders are "female" because they represent an extreme of normal feminine behavior, while antisocial personality disorder marks the extreme of masculinity. Nuckolls's point is not that patients necessarily fit these stereotypes but rather that the categories are "do not go there" signposts and limit-cases for normal gendered behavior patterns.

10. Cf. Ian Hacking, "Making Up People," in *Reconstructing Individualism*, ed. Thomas C. Heller, Morton Sosna, and David E. Wellbery (Stanford: Stanford University Press, 1986).

11. Giorgio Agamben, *Homo Sacer: Sovereign Power and Bare Life*, trans. Daniel Heller-Roazen (Stanford: Stanford University Press, 1998); Louis A. Sass, *Madness and Modernism: Insanity in the Light of Modern Art, Literature and Thought* (New York: Basic Books, 1992).

12. I am not making the argument that the emotional expression signified by "borderline" is compatible with the "schizoid" position but rather—as Sass points out—precisely that it is not.

13. The larger context of these meetings is beyond the scope of this essay, but suffice it to say that custody and treatment perspectives do not easily harmonize; see Rhodes, *Total Confinement: Madness and Reason in the Maximum Security Prison* (Berkeley: University of California Press, 2004).

14. Rebecca Lemov, *World as Laboratory: Experiments with Mice, Mazes and Men*, (New York: Hill and Wang, 2005).

15. An important aspect of this operation is a constant project of writing, distributing, posting and documenting BMAs in an attempt to increase consistency and track effectiveness.

16. Note that while the management agreement must be predictable to work, without desire there is nothing to work on. A nurse said of one inmate who was under restraint for weeks, "He was different from others because *nothing* motivated him—he didn't care about TV, reading, he didn't care about anything. He was very stubborn that way—he had an incredible will."

17. I take this descriptor of the borderline situation from Janice M. Cauwels, *Imbroglio: Rising to the Challenges of Borderline Personality Disorder*, (New York: W. W. Norton and Co, 1992).

13

"Recovery for What?": On Drugs and Psychopharmafetishism

John Marlovits

Publicly, licit and illicit drugs have little in common. Instead, this conjunction is assigned to the prehistory of modern medicine at best, or considered an embarrassing historical accident at worst. If psychopharmacology has disavowed its relationship to discredited prescription practices, drugs, and patent medicines, it has only done so insofar as pharmaceutical companies have been able to remake drugs—including opiates, tranquilizers, and amphetamines—with slight molecular modifications, and package them as scientific medicine.

For example, drugs like Ritalin or certain diet pills are very closely related in chemical composition to amphetamine. The action of a drug like Ritalin, and even some of its effects, differ very little from amphetamines, but cultural ideologies, rituals of ingestion, and technologies of delivery vary considerably. This is to say that drugs are not completely pharmacologically determined, and the brains they affect do not sit disembodied in vats. On the contrary, cultural expectations and the cultivation of the senses and body contribute to the understanding and experience of the effects of drugs.

Errata

The following references were inadvertently omitted from the essay *"Recovery for What?": On Drugs and Psychopharmafetishism* by John Marlovits, p. 104. Reference locations are indicated in square brackets after each note.

Notes

1. This paper benefited greatly from conversations with Hugh Raffles, Susan Harding, Nancy Chen, Mark Anderson, and Megan Moodie. I also want to thank Helene Moglen for her insightful editorial advice. [page 104, title]

2. Richard DeGrandpre, "Constructing the Pharmacological," *Capitalism/Nature/Socialism* 13(1): 2002. [p. 104, paragraph 1]

3. For an interesting ethnographic example, see Nina Etkin, "Side-Effects: Cultural Constructions and Reinterpretations of Western Pharmaceuticals," *Medical Anthropology Quarterly* 6(2): 99–113. [p. 104, par. 2]

4. João Biehl, *Vita: Life in a Zone of Social Abandonment* (Berkeley: University of California Press, 2005). [p. 106, par. 1]

5. See Aiwha Ong, *Buddha Is Hiding: Refugees, Citizenship, the New America* (Berkeley: University of California Press, 2003). [p. 106, par. 1 (US–Southeast Asian history)]

6. American Psychiatric Association, *The Diagnostic and Statistical Manual, IV* (Washington, DC: American Psychiatric Association, 1994). [p. 106, par. 2 (DSM IV)]

7. See Lorna Rhodes, *Emptying Beds: The Work of an Emergency Psychiatric Unit* (Berkeley: University of California Press, 1991) for a discussion of the pragmatics of diagnosis in specific institutions—specifically, in an emergency unit. [p. 108, par. 1]

8. Michel Foucault, *Discipline and Punish*, Alan Sheridan, trans. (New York: Vintage, 1977). [p. 108, par. 2 (docile bodies)]

9. Vilma Santiago-Irizarry, *Medicalizing Ethnicity: The Construction of Latino Identity in a Psychiatric Setting* (Ithaca: Cornell University Press, 2001). [p. 108, par. 2 ("ambience therapy")]

10. Anna Tsing, "How To Make Resources in Order to Destroy Them (and Then Save Them?) on the Salvage Frontier," in *Histories of the Future*, Daniel Rosenberg and Susan Harding, eds. (Durham: Duke University Press, 2005). [p. 110, par. 3]

11. The phrase is Bruno Latour's. See *Pandora's Hope: Essays on the Reality of Science Studies* (Cambridge: Harvard, 1999). [p. 111, par. 1 ("the brain in a vat")]

12. The concept of the pharmakon comes from Jacques Derrida, *Dissemination,* trans. Barbara Johnson. (Chicago: University of Chicago Press, 1982). [p. 111, par. 2 (counter-pharmakon)]

13. There are a number of works that address this topic. See Caroline Jean Acker, *Creating the American Junkie: Addiction Research in the Classic Era of Narcotic Control* (Baltimore: Johns Hopkins, 2002); David Courtwright, *Dark Paradise: A History of Opiate Addiction in America,* second edition (Cambridge: Harvard, 2001); Curtis Marez, *Drug Wars: The Political Economy of Narcotics* (Minneapolis: University of Minnesota Press, 2004); Joseph Spillane, *Cocaine: From Medical Marvel to Modern Menace in the United States, 1884–1920* (Baltimore: Johns Hopkins, 2000). [p. 111, par. 2 (urban decay)]

14. Richard DeGrandpre, "Constructing the Pharmacological." [p. 111, par. 2 ("the differential production of drugs")]

15. Curtis Marez, *Drug Wars.* [p. 111, par. 2 ("the management of drug traffic")]

16. See Alexander Cockburn and Jeffrey St. Clair, *Whiteout: The CIA, Drugs, and the Press* (London: Verso, 1998). [p. 111, par. 2 (in Laos)]

17. See David Healy, *The Antidepressant Era* (Cambridge: Harvard University Press, 1997), especially chapter 4. [p. 112, par. 1 (anti-pychotics)]

18. Foucault, *Madness and Civilization,* Richard Howard, trans. (New York: Vintage, 1965). [p. 112. par. 2 (". . . the inside of the outside")]

This brief paper has two goals that I will pursue by drawing on my field research in two so-called culturally sensitive community mental health centers that cater to lower or underclass groups in Seattle. First, it shows how drug discourse shapes the application of psychopharmaceuticals in community mental health clinics in ways that construct a liminal, passive subject position—rather than an actively recovering client. In other words, I will show how the use of psychopharmaceuticals constructs the search for mental health as a temporality of perpetual waiting and deferred expectations. Second, I want to examine the contradictory ways that psychopharmacological practice is employed to combat the use of illicit drugs and drug addiction, while—in so doing—it contains and disavows pharmacology's past in legacies of the Vietnam and Cold War eras, and bolsters an implicitly normative model of white minds and bodies. I will begin with a few brief vignettes.

Army Surplus

I met two clients while volunteering in a day program for Asian Americans, Noi and Pravat. Noi was a Laotian refugee. He regularly wore military clothing: camouflage jackets, military caps, shirts, even marine slacks with a white stripe down the leg. Sometimes he would wear military dress shoes—the latter, as one staffer pointed out to me, not a matching pair. But Noi could look strangely official even if he was obviously wearing army surplus clothes. Staffers at the center spoke about the fact that he was an incredible mimic, particularly of other languages—even though he only really spoke Mien.

In addition to his playful antics, Noi's attire was generally considered as evidence of his mental illness. Even if he was widely appreciated, and his antics enjoyed (he drank water from small plastic liquor bottles that one might get on a plane, for example, and had a highly personal artistic signature), his behavior was still considered to be a sign of his irrationality rather than a world-making enterprise in its own right. Much less did his obvious interest in and performance of militarization register as bearing any relation to mental illness—except as proof of it. "His voice," as João Biehl has put it, "was annulled by psychiatric diagnosis." Rather than address the complexities of cross-cultural trauma, Noi's dislocation, and the history of US–Southeast Asian history, Noi's circumstances and his capabilities were reductively conceptualized in terms of a seemingly objective scientific logic organized mostly on the basis of case studies of people who were nothing like him.

Cleaning the Temple

While the history of the Vietnam war was registered in the materiality of Noi's attire, it was registered in other ways with another client—a young man in his thirties named Pravat. The staff member in charge of the day program became annoyed with Pravat on a number of occasions while I was volunteering. Pravat constantly made efforts to clean the room in which the program was run, would try to straighten up the shelves, clean the floor, arrange some of the games. He was asked multiple times to stop, but he kept it up—of course, he didn't speak English. Annoyed, the staff supervisor was convinced that his behavior was evidence of Obsessive-Compulsive Disorder, and a psychiatric nurse and Pravat's case manager were called in to discuss the case with the staff. The staff, case managers, the psychiatric nurse, and I compared notes about Pravat, debating which diagnosis fit and whether he needed to be medicated for OCD. The psychiatric nurse was unconvinced that OCD was the right diagnosis, though the staff member in charge lobbied hard for her own position. We all pulled out the DSM IV and consulted it. The case manager added that Pravat had outbursts resembling conversion hysteria in his office when he didn't get his way. I got the feeling, though, that communication with Pravat was difficult or unclear, and that there were power struggles behind the scenes. For instance, Pravat lived with another man, and from time to time the two of them would get angry at the case workers at our clinic and start going to the Latina/o clinic in Seattle.

What became most striking to me, though, was Pravat's background. Pravat was generally considered a Thai client. His case manager spoke Thai. But while nationality organized client support, Pravat's national origin was not so simple, and I suspect the same held true for his linguistic skills. From what the psychiatric nurse reconstructed of Pravat's background, I found out that Pravat had been born somewhere near the border of Vietnam shortly before the beginning of the war. As a child he was orphaned after witnessing his parents' murder. In the aftermath, Pravat somehow found his way into the hands of a Buddhist monastery. His job was to clean the temple.

Ambience Therapy on an Internalized Frontier

Given this information about the traumatic nature of Pravat's past and the cultural dislocations he experienced, efforts to diagnose and re-diagnose him seemed out of joint. Moreover, I couldn't help but be struck by the possibility that he wanted something to do, that contrary to how his actions were perceived, he was demonstrating a desire to work.

However, the process that the staff went through in order to have his illness evaluated participated in the common logic or protocol of psychiatric practice in the clinic. In this case, Pravat began to act up and, within the interpretive frame of the clinic, his actions forced a consideration of his illness and hence his medication—his misbehavior was a potential symptom. The reason for considering re-diagnosing him with OCD was related to the staff's effort to provide him with appropriate drugs. Antidepressants are indicated for OCD, and therefore re-diagnosing him might lead to better drug treatment and the disappearance of his symptoms.

When I began my fieldwork in the clinic, I asked the staff person in charge a number of questions about the symptoms of illness and how one learned to spot them. Most of these questions irritated my interlocutor, who typically brushed me off by handing me the DSM, or answering that she "saw people, not diagnoses." Fair enough. Of course, on the contrary, I began to notice that any kind of misbehavior in our daily sessions was interpreted as a sign of mental illness—even if it was unclear which illness it was—which puts "seeing people, not diagnoses" in a different light. The mandate of the organization was focused on trying to "stabilize" clients, which is to say keep them from de-compensating or having a psychotic episode and ending up in psychiatric hospitals. So while recovery was an ideal concept, practice—and the use of psychopharmaceuticals—was implicitly oriented more towards anxieties over de-compensation. In other words, the concept of mental illness was embedded in the institutional ecology between clinics and emergency wards as well as in the disciplinary strategies of the clinic.

The seeming insignificance of Pravat's actions demonstrated the kinds of disciplinary procedures at work in the center through which the signs of mental health and illness are articulated. Interventions were made with clients who acted out in some way, but not to clients who were passive—even frighteningly passive, as can become the case with antipsychotic agents. Moreover, the dominant mood of the program was downright boredom, on the part both of clients and staff, a dominant mood that I came to see as quite central—rather than incidental—to its disciplinary strategies. This boredom, which I understood as part and parcel of the production of docile bodies, was based in what Vilma Santiago-Irizarry calls "ambience therapy." Mental health is treated like something of an ambience, a sort of baseline or natural state that, in the absence of obstructions, will manifest itself in a zen-like—or perhaps more appropriately, a leisurely—calm. The general state of boredom in the clinic was perceived as a calm, therapeutic environment, a calm that Pravat was seen as both disrupting and lacking. Finally, this calm was produced through the conjunction of observational practices and ideologies of psychopharmaceuticals—what I want to call an institutionally specific form of psychopharmafetishism.

This sense of boredom and waiting was also articulated by several African-American informants at a different community mental health center to which I now turn.

Whose Side?

"I fought in the Vietnam war," Kenneth told me. "I ended up there because I got busted by the cops and had to go to court. The judge told me that I could either go to jail, or I could enlist in the army—so I enlisted. That's really when I started getting heavily into drugs. When I was in Vietnam I remember being stationed outside of enemy lines. The Vietnamese army would play these recordings over loudspeakers in broken English. They would say something like 'Hey black men, why are you fighting us? We've never done anything to you. We don't hate you. We don't call you ugly names.' I remember listening to that and being like, 'Damn, those guys are right.'"

For years after returning from Vietnam, Kenneth was embroiled in the cocaine economy of Pioneer Square, the neighborhood once known as "skid row," a term that refers both to the road used to slide logs to Henry Yesler's mill on Elliott Bay and to the red-light district that grew up around it and catered to Seattle's migrant laborers. On and off, Kenneth lived between the Morrison Hotel in Pioneer Square, a psychiatric center that struck me as a postwar parallel to the old dime and quarter motels that used to line First Avenue—the old skid row—to house migrant laborers. When he made enough cash selling drugs, he stayed in cheap motel rooms way up Highway 99 on the northern edge of the city.

Kenneth had been diagnosed with a variety of illnesses over time—PTSD, Multiple Personality Disorder, bipolar disorder. He had been seeking care for thirteen years at the mental health clinic where we met, although he claimed that it was only in the past two years that he had decided to "take his recovery seriously." By that, he not only meant giving up drugs and alcohol—which brought out his other personalities, as his wife once told me. He also became actively engaged in what was considered the work of recovery—much of which consisted of talking about his illness and circumstances in particular ways.

Kenneth would narrate his recovery as a conversion experience, adopting the language and narratives of mental health. He courted mental health discourse in order to break from his past and to give shape to a possible future but, at the same time, he was acutely aware that the language of mental health assumed a passivity and loss of agency, a catch-22, that was remarkably similar to the one he confronted in dealing drugs. In frustration he reflected on the counterintuitive ways in which drug dealing had actually afforded him more room for maneuver than his recovery, and he searched for strategies that would enable him to resist the passivity that mental health discourse implicitly imposed on him.

Kenneth and his wife Cora registered their resistance to this imposed passivity in their complaints about the lack of appropriate services at their clinic and the ways the clinic had actually obstructed their efforts to organize a lobbying and advocacy organization among the clients. They sometimes mocked the notion of "recovery" because of the way it only created a place of waiting, always waiting to recover. "Recovery?! Recovery for what?! There's not any reason to recover. What am I recovering to?! At least when I was getting high I was getting high."

The comment is telling: there was nowhere to recover to. Recovery was not a goal to reach, but a subjective state itself or, one could say, a subject position produced through the techniques of ambience therapy. This state of passive waiting is, I would argue, a sort of internalized frontier. As Anna Tsing has argued, a frontier is "not simply a place," but "an imaginative project." "Frontiers," she writes, "are not just discovered at the edge; they are projects in making geographic and temporal experience." Recovery for Kenneth was a temporality of uncertainty, a structural position of inadequate support, an anxious waiting room with no exits or lines of flight—except, perhaps, the one he was trying to get away from: drugs.

Kenneth worked hard to get into the space of recovery. His conversion involved both a retelling of his life and a learning of new styles of self-discipline that he demonstrated by organizing his lobbying organization and attending National Alliance for the

Mentally Ill meetings. But his recovery also brought out serious questions about some forms of agency he lost in the process of coming closer to "well." The lobbying group was hard to start without money or a place to meet, and his and Cora's efforts were received with suspicion and paternalism by the clinic staff. Discussion of their circumstances in the lobbying group might include allusions to unsavory aspects of their behavior, like drug use or prostitution, which were considered signs that they were not taking recovery seriously. Indeed, becoming mentally healthy was a matter of ignoring their situated material and cultural circumstances and speaking a disembodied language of mental health in a vacuum, "the brain in a vat." This was what came out not only in their commentaries about recovery, but also in the surfacing of Kenneth's ambivalent nostalgia for the vibrancy of street life and for some of his financial successes in dealing cocaine.

Kenneth's situation also demonstrates the way psychopharmacology functions as a counter-pharmakon, or anti-drug drug. This is not coincidental. Narcotics laws and licit pharmacological drugs arose in response to the increasing racialization of drugs in the early twentieth century, which was due to anxieties over immigration and urban decay, and which resulted in what DeGrandpre calls "the differential production of drugs." In other words, the traffic between or the transgression of licit/illicit boundaries has been common both in scientific work and in diplomacy, which Curtis Marez has urged us to see not as "drug enforcement" but as "the management of drug traffic." For instance, it is well known that drug use was rampant among American GIs in Vietnam, and that American forces actively supported drug operations like General Vang Pao's in Laos. Similarly, it is generally known that LSD was considered for its potential as a mind control drug. It may be less well known, however, that it also provided the research model—the "model psychosis"—that, taken up by psychopharmacologists, contributed to the elucidation of models of neurotransmission as well as to the development of antidepressants and anti-psychotics. My point is not simply that this puts licit and illicit drugs into conversation, but that licit drugs work off the contrast with illicit drugs so that they are able to imply purity, morality, and an implicit view of the proper subject. Taking psychopharmaceuticals means participating in a collective imagination of a cultural ideal: it is not merely a matter of chemistry.

Moreover, the historical specificities of psychopharmacology are firmly placed within the postwar era, when they not only produced ways of containing behavior but also shaped ways of understanding the predicaments of people like Kenneth, Pravat, and Noi. My point in juxtaposing these three individuals, their important differences aside, is to demonstrate their positioning in and their containment by the internalized frontier of community mental health. They are positioned, to borrow from Foucault, "on the outside of the inside and the inside of the outside." This inside/outside is the frontier space of ambience therapy, psychopharmafetishism, and a model of mental health implicitly based on middle-class imaginaries. Ambience therapy not only mimics leisure; it also attempts to model an appropriate private sphere—symbolized most strongly in the "clubhouse" spaces designed to reproduce living rooms in community mental health centers. This subjectivity is also modeled in the refusal of mental health workers to engage with the situated constraints of individuals like Kenneth. Although these clients are seemingly included, attended to, and rehabilitated, the ambience therapy to which they are subject nevertheless reinforces their not-quite-middle-class-citizen status.

Finally, it is no coincidence that illicit and licit drugs meet in this space precisely because drugs construct an intermediate place where postwar America faces its external and internal others. In dealing cocaine, not to mention fighting in Vietnam, Kenneth was positioned at the intersection of the black and white markets of global capitalism—again, an inside/outside phenomenon. In turning away from illicit drugs and embracing his recovery, he was surprised to find how little difference exists between the two options. Mental health and psychopharmacology, in this perspective, turn out to look like a forced cultural imaginary, seemingly holding out the promise of support on the basis of drugs produced and developed through exclusionary racial and national ideologies.

To close, I remember asking the staff supervisor I worked with about the problems, and even abuse, that our clients faced. Her response, professional and annoyed as usual, was "yes, but we ask that you not talk to the clients about that."

14

The Other Inside

Carla Freccero

Psychoanalytic theories of subjectivity argue that subjectivity—the experience of thinking feeling embodiment—is, first and foremost, intersubjectivity, a relation to an other. In "Mourning and Melancholia," the essay that most vividly evokes the figure of "the other inside," Freud describes melancholia—the continued and ambivalent attachment to an object perceived to be lost—as a kind of incorporation, the taking in of the lost object so that it persists within the self and is preserved.[1] Later, in *The Ego and the Id*, he extends the melancholic model and suggests that the ego itself is the "precipitate" of all the attachments to objects loved and then lost, that the ego sublimates its attachment to—and contains the history of—lost others, who are taken up as identifications (ego ideals, for example).[2] In another imaginative configuration of this other inside, Nicolas Abraham and Maria Torok use the metaphor of the tomb within the self—the encrypted object—to describe the fantasmatic melancholic incorporation of a lost other.[3] There are various applications of this model to other modes of identitarian embodiment. Judith Butler, for example, argues that gender is formed by melancholically taking on the same-sex object of love, that in a homophobic culture we identify with (that is, we become)—so as not to lose—the forbidden and thus foreclosed same-sex attachment. We cannot have our same-sex parent, so we become him or her, and this gets extended to the social scale of gender as an organizing system.[4] Jay Prosser aligns the subjectivity of the transsexual with the desire of the internalized other sex to emerge from within the prison of its differently engendered/sexed skin, while Anne Anlin Cheng claims that there is a melancholia of race, and that "white American identity and its authority is [sic] secured through the melancholic introjection of racial others that it can neither fully relinquish nor accommodate and whose ghostly presence nonetheless guarantees its centrality."[5] Indeed, Jacques Derrida notes that our whole network of intersubjective relations could be described according to the metaphorics of orality and ingestion, from the taking in of the breast of the mother in nursing to the communion of speaking and listening to another's words. He calls this "the dominant schema of subjectivity itself" in Western, "carno-phallogocentric," culture.[6]

This paper explores what it means to conceive of and experience embodied subjectivity as an alien inhabitation—most often violent and hostile—and what it means to experience the other as inside, to say that "I" and "me," both "selves" if you will, are strangers to each other even in their neighboring proximity. If subjectivity comes into being through the imaginative or fantasmatic taking in of what is alien, outside, be it understood as an other or the world, how does this inhabitation live on in the subject? And how might this way of thinking about subjectivity inform a politics of relationality?

Science fiction and horror are a good place to look for imaginative popular figurations of this incorporative notion of embodied subjectivity. They are genres that, on the one hand, experiment with alternative worlds and, on the other, tap deep into primal fears, literalizing them in narratives about monsters. I have chosen the Alien series for its obvious resonances with the problem I outline here, and for the fact that it is both science fiction and horror. I choose it also because the "human" subjectivity it explores is feminine—that is, its privileged human protagonist is a woman, Sigourney Weaver as

Ripley—and because the series is about biological reproduction, enabling it to deploy the most literal and normative merging of alien and self—pregnancy—as the privileged terrain for figuring a horrifying defamiliarization. Finally, as a series that extends over several decades, employing several directors but keeping similar narrative premises intact, it also can be read as an allegory of differing ideological—national and cultural—fantasies about subjectivity and the relation between "self" and "other" that takes the form, I argue, of a certain thinking about the question of the human.

In the first movie (1979), titled *Alien* and directed by Ridley Scott, Ripley (Sigourney Weaver) and her gang discover a planet inhabited by alien creatures that implant themselves in human hosts in order to reproduce.[7] These aliens are only partly organic matter; they have "acid" for blood and are able over time to convert into inorganic material. The meditation on the question of the human thus begins immediately for, as it turns out, one of the "human" company is himself not entirely organic, but an android (he has "milk" for blood), and it is he who most ardently loves, praises and admires the unusual hybrid composition of the beautifully adapted creature. The birth scene in this film is a masculine one and thus seems far removed from the unsettling thought that the very condition of embodiment for humans may entail, at some point in our lives, the hostile inhabitation of or by an other. In this movie, the bugs are bugs, parasites that feed on us and kill us. Here then the meditation on the human takes the form of the "monkey's paw" parable that warns us that technological prosthetic enhancements to the human exact their cost. The corporation (called simply "the company") is attempting to invest in the incorporation of aliens for weapons research and development. The ego ideal of the android is a hostile other indeed, bent on humanity's demise. At the end of the movie humanity is preserved from that contamination. Or so we think.

In the second movie, far more reactionary and yet also cleverer in its social punning than the first, *Aliens*, the horrific fantasy is brought home to roost with Ripley's nightmare of giving birth to one of the aliens via traumatic cesarean, where the alien bursts through the chest of the host. Further—and uglier—the narrative centers on a battle between mothers— Ripley as adoptive mother to an abandoned girl called Newt versus the alien mother herself, a queen, black and teeming with masses of eggs ready to colonize white bodies and the world. Our first-world military feminist heroine annihilates the "bitch" with superior firepower and an exoskeleton that resembles a hummer crossed with a forklift. That was the mid-eighties, after all (1986).The film makers are *Terminator's* James Cameron and his wife. The alien, both inside and out, had come to have widespread national popular resonance and was the target of muscular xenophobia. Whereas the first movie had featured the usual heroic working-class black man who dies nobly for the cause while protecting his white charges, and its concept of "alien" had to do with the mixture of the organic and the technological in a reference to oil as the product and enabling source of organic life, this film puns instead on "alien" in its reference to two groups of people in particular: Latinos (the heroic Marine who dies saving others' lives is Latina, her name is Vasquez, and she is stereotypically butch) and Asians (the labels on the military industrial equipment belonging to the Wayland-Yutani corporation are in Japanese). The theme of aliens is extended as an imperialist fantasy, so that not only are there aliens within, but the aliens without are threatening our borders too, threatening the U.S. with the possibility of being no longer human.

There is a long story about how those aliens came to inhabit the planet in question—we are told they are settler colonies, rather than the indigenous inhabitants of the planet that the "company" is in the process of "terraforming." The heroes of this movie—in addition to Ripley—are the Marines. *Aliens* also has an android, but instead of being evil, this one is good, suffering evisceration at the hands of the aliens in order to rescue Ripley and Newt. The fear of nature taking revenge on humanity for its bio-technological progress has all but disappeared. Much is made of Ripley's relationship to one of the Marines in charge of the expedition; Ripley, Newt and this guy seem to become, by the movie's end, the new nuclear family. The director's cut makes explicit the metaphor of childbirth by having Newt point out that the aliens seem to be born the same way. This is thus a film that links together whiteness (disavowed by the extreme multicultural multiracial composition of the Marines), the nuclear family, the military industrial complex, and US imperialism, against the threat of invasion and consumption by inhuman massively reproducing and threatening aliens, staged as a story about competing maternal ferocities. It ends, like the previous film, with the purging and re-purification of humanity.

The third film in the series, *Alien³*, released in 1992, changes the terms of the meditation on embodied subjectivity as a hostile and violent alien inhabitation. At the beginning of the movie, Ripley's new family is summarily killed off as she crash-lands on a remote planet, Fury (Fiorina) 161, functioning as a maximum security "yy" facility. We are inside the prison industrial complex, and, in this movie, there is no outside. This time we watch the alien being born from the body of a dog, so that it loses its specificity as an other (human) subject, becoming "merely" non-human, and as if to say, too, that our best friend has now become our enemy. The metaphorics of this film reference the culture of AIDS, from a scene of the names of the dead being read off by the ship's log like the famous Names project, to the look of the prisoners, to the "yy" signifier of the all-male enclave, to the slogans as the prisoners begin to organize collectively to confront their fate and change the future. It also seems to reference and echo the words of Diamanda Galas, "we are all HIV positive," for while the alien invades a population of rejected and marginal men, some of whom are rapists and murderers, others of whom are heroin addicts, it also affects everywoman—Ripley. The movie suggests that this is what is left of our world, or rather, that there is no longer an outside perspective from which we could identify and purge the alien within. Ripley learns that she is pregnant and, in a scene as erotic as it is horrifying, we watch the alien recognize her as its kin. When she determines to seek it out and kill it, she tells one of the prisoners: "I'm going to look for it in the basement." He retorts: "What do you mean, this whole place is a basement!" And, in a clever *mise-en-abîme* of the genre as whole, and the Alien series in particular, she replies, "it's a metaphor," pointing to the alien's spatial location in the unconscious. Seeking it out, she croons, "Don't be afraid; I'm part of the family," and "You've been in my life so long, I can't remember anything else." The hostile inhabitation by an alien other whose provenance is manifestly elsewhere in the first two movies has finally mutated, and, though no less frightening for being uncannily familiar, the alien's indwelling is melancholic rather than phobic. In the end, the prisoners display a futile heroism in their attempt to save the world from themselves—and we are to understand the gesture as beautiful, poignant, and pointless. Ripley, pregnant with the possibility of a shiny new weapon in the war on everyone, dives into a pit of molten lead with her arms in the shape of a cross, later clutching her baby to her breast as it is born screaming from her chest. The mood is elegiac, gloomy, resigned. Everyone dies, with the exception of a minor character who is carted off by the company, which arrives serendipitously too late to rescue the prisoners from their fate. One of the last lines in the movie, uttered by this prisoner, is "Fuck you!"

But there's one more movie to consider: *Alien:Resurrection*. As the final image of the 1992 film suggests, Ripley is a postmodern Jesus, sacrificing herself to save a humanity that is already doomed. She is ironically reborn in 1997 as an unnaturally tall, unnaturally strong alien human hybrid, living on a spaceship that is an experimental science station. A motley crew of space merchants and pirates arrive on the ship, including a strong man, a legless dwarf, a pretty young girl who's also tough (Winona Ryder), and a handsome rogue for a captain. These are mostly the actors Jean-Pierre Jeunet casts in his other strange movies about marginals, *The City of Lost*

Children and *Delicatessen* (this was before Jeunet's crossover *Amélie* movie days). They have been charged with the delivery of clandestine cargo, and we soon find out what that cargo is and why. Scientists on the ship have been breeding aliens: we see adult aliens in high-tech prison cells and a kind of organic factory where the human hosts the pirates have delivered are held captive for the alien eggs to implant themselves within and hatch. The scientists have extracted the queen from Ripley—she is the one churning out those eggs—and Ripley herself turns out to be the perfected recombinant DNA experiment.

The "xeno-morphs" break loose, and Ripley, still willing to protect what's left of humanoid life in the world, suggests that the crew destroy the ship and escape. Along the way we learn by surprise that Annalee Call, the girl pirate, is herself an android, and she comes in for a lot of scorn as a result, though here xenophobia of any kind is manifestly ironic, since both Ryder and Weaver are the stars of the movie, and since apart from the misshapen and primitive marginals who rescue themselves and the ship, the only "good" guys are no longer human. Ripley and Call immediately become friends, recognizing their alternative kinship—though Annalee, as the "good" post-human, was supposed to destroy Ripley, the supposedly bad post-human—and together they plan the escape of the pirates. Destination? Earth. "That shit-hole?," one of the crew says.

At the center of this film there is a scene: Ripley, searching for the aliens, comes upon a room full of botched experiments in jars, a museum of monstrosities. She sees a badly deformed woman chained down in a bed, begging to be killed. This woman's hybridization has failed where Ripley's has succeeded; she is the mirror image whose monstrosity has been rendered explicitly visible. In anguish, Ripley does as she asks, torching the entire room in the process. I wonder if this is the end of melancholia and the beginning of mourning, this moment when Ripley purges herself of her attachment to the loss-rendered material, palpable, visible, by her mirrored monster self.

Before the group's final escape, Ripley senses a disturbance in the alien queen. She returns to the queen's lair to comfort her because the queen is in pain. The hybridization process has worked both ways and the queen is in labor, giving birth, finally, in the way that a human woman does, rather than laying eggs. The child she births is a son, humanoid and alien at once, horrifyingly huge and infantile—premature—in the way human babies are. He immediately recognizes Ripley as his Mom, hating and then killing his birth mother because of her alien ugliness. He also, predictably, gets on board the escape pod with the survivors. In a scene as horrifying as it is moving, Ripley coos maternally at the monster, luring him to an open hatch in the ship till he gets sucked out into space, screaming. This comic and lurid imitation of abortion techniques clinches the metaphorics of pregnancy, alien inhabitation, and abortion that the film has been weaving together. Ripley, representative of the new post-human order of hybrid organic/non-organic life, occupies both poles of the abortion question, vigorously affirming maternal possession while also dispensing with the products of her genetic material for the sake of a better world. Interestingly, the movie allows us both to feel compassion and sympathy for the baby monster and the monster mother on the one hand, and to understand the necessity for their deaths in the logic of the plot, on the other, for the "alien" instinct is to kill all other life forms and consume them.

Ripley, who should be scripted as a monster for the devious and brutal way she murders her child, is, though inhuman, the heroine and focalized subjectivity of the tale. The alien/human that she is is as fully violent and dangerous as the pure alien was—so it's not a sentimentalization or domestication of the notion of the alien within—but this time the alien inhabitation (and at this point inhabitation as a metaphor becomes completely inadequate) is familiar. She recognizes herself as other. Thus instead of remaining within the unconscious, or secretly encrypted within the self, lurking in the basement, ready to strike out at its human prey—and thus justifying the massive projection of alterity onto an outside other world, as a hostile alien requiring annihilation—the other that is the self can make judgments and alliances grounded in a different logic, a logic of what may be conceptually undecidable but requiring choice nevertheless. An ethical logic, we could call it.

As they approach earth, that blue, green, brown and white ball we're so accustomed to from every ecology poster that also sports the slogan, "Love your Mother," the very last lines of the movie are an exchange between the android Call, who's never seen it, and Ripley. Annalee says, "It's beautiful," and Ripley says, "Yeah." Call then continues, "I didn't expect it to be. What happens now?" Ripley replies, "I don't know. I'm a stranger here myself." The inheritors of the earth have never been there, they are post-human creatures resembling and inheriting something of the human without themselves being human.

So what might this late twentieth-century popular representation have to say about the question of the human, its future, and the politics of relationality? On the one hand, it seems to say we are not fully, wholly, purely, ourselves: we are occupied by or occupy a hostile, frightening other who is alien to the reassuring fiction of the human we've created as our "self-" understanding. In the words of the title of Donna Haraway's announced conference presentation, we are not—perhaps have never been—human. We are organic-inorganic, genetic trans-species hybrids. We cannot choose between our "self" and the "other" inside, for we are both. And whereas this split subjectivity can be understood as threatening, as unleashing a murderous rivalry, it can also be understood, as *Alien: Resurrection* shows, as the impossibility of inhabiting the purely human in order to destroy, annihilate, purge, the other. *Alien: Resurrection*—a post-human manifesto if ever there was one—urges us to recognize the inability to locate and isolate the other inside because that other does not live outside but is the constitutive otherness, whether physical or psychic, of ourselves for ourselves and others. But—and here I think about how much of the collection highlights normativizing regimes of appearance—US mass-mediated popular forms of cultural production like this nevertheless retain their gossamer attachment to high Western humanist regulatory norms of embodiment, for the new post-human race, like the Time or Newsweek magazine cover representing the racially, ethnically, and gender morphed human of the future, must still look a lot like "us."

Notes

1. Sigmund Freud, "Mourning and Melancholia (1917)," in *General Psychological Theory: Papers on Metapsychology*, trans. Joan Riviere, ed. Philip Rieff (New York: Simon and Schuster, 1991, repr. 1997), pp. 164-179. Jacques Derrida makes the point that in some ways melancholia can be understood as the effort to preserve an ethical relation to the lost other, since to mourn successfully is to kill the loved object yet again. But, as he also adds, that melancholic attachment itself is a betrayal, since what is preserved is a fantasmatic version of that other anyway. See Jacques Derrida and Elisabeth Roudinesco, *For What Tomorrow . . . A Dialogue*, trans. Jeff Fort (Stanford, CA: Stanford University Press, 2004), esp. pp. 159-60.

2. For Freud the ego is always a bodily ego; there is a relay of sensation, felt to emanate both from without and from within. This relay maps a kind of psychic body that usually corresponds to the surface of the skin. See Sigmund Freud, The Ego and the Id, trans. Joan Riviere, ed. James Strachey (New York: Norton, 1960, repr. 1989), esp. p. 20.

3. Nicolas Abraham and Maria Torok, *The Shell and the Kernel*, volume 1, ed. and trans. Nicholas Rand (Chicago: The University of Chicago Press, 1994).

4. See *Gender Trouble: Feminism and the Subversion of Identity* (New York: Routledge, 1990) and *Bodies that Matter: On the Discursive Limits of "Sex"* (New York: Routledge,1993). In *The Psychic Life of Power: Theories in Subjection* (Stanford: Stanford University Press, 1997), Butler further argues that all subjectivity is melancholic, the taking in of our attachment to the world: "The psychic form of reflexivity melancholia elaborates carries the trace of the other within it as a dissimulated sociality . . . The melancholic does not merely withdraw the lost object from consciousness, but withdraws into the psyche a configuration of the social world as well" (p. 181).

5. Jay Prosser, *Second Skins: The Body Narratives of Transsexuality* (New York: Columbia University Press, 1998); Anne Anlin Cheng, *The Melancholy of Race: Psychoanalysis, Assimilation, and Hidden Grief* (New York: Oxford University Press, 2001), p. xi.

6. Jacques Derrida, "'Eating Well,' or the Calculation of the Subject," in *Points . . . Interviews, 1974-1994*, trans. Peggy Kamuf et al., ed. Elisabeth Weber (Stanford, CA: Stanford University Press, 1995): pp. 255-287, at p. 281.

7. The four films in question are: *Alien*, dir. Ridley Scott (Twentieth Century Fox/Brandywine, 1979); *Aliens*, dir. James Cameron (Twentieth Century Fox/Brandywine, 1986); *Alien*[3], dir. David Fincher (Twentieth Century Fox/Brandywine, 1992); and *Alien: Resurrection*, dir. Jean-Pierre Jeunet (Twentieth Century Fox/Brandywine, 1997).

IV

Social Bodies
and Transformation

15

Aged Bodies and Kinship Matters: The Biologization of Moral Commitment[1]

Sharon R. Kaufman, Ann J. Russ and Janet K. Shim

Renal transplantation has emerged as the treatment of choice for medically suitable patients with end-stage renal disease. More than 60,000 patients await kidney transplantation and are listed on the United Network for Organ Sharing (UNOS) recipient registry. Live donor renal transplantation represents the most promising solution for closing the gap between organ supply and demand.

Journal of the American Medical Association, 2005[2]

One of the effects of contemporary medicine, from a sociopolitical point of view, is to place death within a framework of ethical decision-making that emphasizes the fight against specific mortal diseases and conditions.³ In the United States, more than in any other country, routine clinical practices often ignore the inevitability of biological senescence in old age that eventually leads to death, and few moral, legal or (so it often appears) financial barriers exist to halt interventions that treat 'end-stage disease' as sustainable or even reversible. The activities that constitute clinical life extension, like so many other medical practices, comprise a site for the governing of life and relationships and the emergence of new forms of social participation in which biological knowledge and identification are foregrounded. Our ethnographic example at this site is kidney transplantation for older adults and we ask, what kind of subjectification emerges when longevity at older ages becomes an object of intervention and apparent choice?

We are concerned with how family and other relationships are implicated in a biopolitical field in which certain medical practices (along with their legitimating financial supports), and the desire for and expectation of a longer life, and changing ideas about "normal" old age, and family obligation become intertwined. The substance of the body, as ground for moral consideration, stands out as a dominant cultural feature in this example. So we are exploring the kinds of social obligations and thus, moral order,⁴ at stake and in play when the age for transplant moves up beyond seventy and, especially, when living donors come from the succeeding generation.

The number of kidneys transplanted to people over age sixty-five, both from live and cadaver donors, has increased steadily in the past two decades in the United States. Transplants are routine in the seventh decade of life and sometimes are performed into the early eighties. Cadaver kidneys from donors over age fifty are sought and are available so that they can ease the shortage of transplantable kidneys for older recipients. In addition, living kidney donation is on the rise for all age groups, exceeding cadaver donation for the first time in the United States in 2001. In our own observational context, adult children (in their thirties, forties and fifties) are donating kidneys to their parents (currently, those who are in their sixties and seventies). Nephews and nieces, spouses, other relatives and friends are donating kidneys to older persons as well.

The "tyranny of the gift"[5] Fox and Swazey describe—the imperative to offer and give, accept and receive the gift of an organ and the gift of a longer life, regardless of health or suffering, guilt or desire—has additional moral and social ramifications when the direction of organ transfer is from younger to older persons. That tyranny is marked by a sense among some recipients that this direction of transfer is unnatural, and by a sense among some health professionals and others that this direction of transfer is inappropriate from the standpoint of medical goals and use of resources. Yet many recipients feel obligated to live for their families, and donors feel duty-bound to allow their parent (or older relative or friend) to continue living—and to facilitate that continued life.

The gift is "not a big deal," we were often told by donors after the fact, because medical technique has made kidney donation ordinary, easy and of negligible risk to the donor. Among recipients there is much more ambivalence about it. Often, recipients' desires to refuse the gift is muted, masked and overwhelmed by the routine-ness of accepting, the discomfort or refusal of dialysis, increasing serious illness, the willingness, enthusiasm and persuasion of a donor and the medical truth that a living donor will provide the best health outcome. These are powerful influences on what happens in the clinic.

Our theme is the consequences of the normalization of kidney transplantation as a clinical/cultural practice. The biomedical truth about the social worth and clinical efficacy of kidney transplantation operates as a cultural system,[6] shaping relationships in the form of an ethic of care. The work done by all players involved is to rationalize and emotionally come to terms with the prospects of offering and giving, accepting and receiving, and, importantly, deciding where one draws the line in networks of family (however defined), friends, and strangers and across relationships that are marked, in the case of relatedness, by protection, love, obligation, and indebtedness and, in the case of strangers or casual acquaintances, by apparent altruism and its acceptance. In one sense, living donor transplantation joins the new reproductive technologies in expanding the field of moral action to include proactive deliberation about the uses of one's own body and the uses of the bodies of others to promote new or extended life. But in the case of organ sharing, biology is not mobilized to configure kinship, but rather, biology as corporeal substance in the form of one's own body, becomes the central object in articulating moral claims on another and in deciding what to do.

Recipients

The recipients and prospective recipients we spoke with articulated a broad range of opinion about the need and urgency to ask for and accept an organ, the obligation not to ask and not to take, and the responsibility either to wait years for a cadaver donor or to quickly solicit one's own potential living donors. Neither ethnicity, immigrant status nor gender determined the ethics and practice of seeking or accepting an organ in our small but diverse sample of thirty-three kidney recipients and twenty-eight prospective recipient interviewees.

Mostly, though not exclusively, the difficulty of saying "no" dominated the ethical field and charted the terms of engagement. Some people want a kidney transplant as soon as (or before) they learn they have "end-stage disease" and they line up prospective donors before talking with health professionals about transplantation. For others, the possibility of a transplant (live donor or cadaver) dawns slowly, over a period of weeks, months or years after dialysis begins. The most passive actors are those who never entertain the possibility of a living donor, wait years, and eventually receive a cadaver donor kidney. For example, a seventy-year-old scientist, with a wife and six children, said:

> "When I was diagnosed with kidney failure, the nephrologist decided to put my name on the transplant list, even

though I didn't really have any intention of having a transplant. Then, as long as the hemodialysis was working out, I accepted that as an alternative to transplant. . . . But the reason I went ahead with it was because it was available, it was an option."

People who make proactive decisions of some kind in regard to seeking or accepting a kidney from a living donor express a range of ethical imperatives. From those who refused to accept a live donation we heard, for example:

"I got a cadaver transplant after a three-year wait. I would never ask my son. I had three years of dialysis. I had to."

In contrast, from individuals who actively sought donors, we heard:

"I was willing to be on dialysis and, in the beginning, my doctors did not offer or discuss transplant. When I learned, two years later, that I wouldn't have to wait around on dialysis if I had a live donor, my wife lined up fourteen people who would donate. One of the transplant nurses told me that that was nothing. She's seen people who have lined up a hundred prospective donors. You have to be proactive. You can't just sit around, or you'll die waiting."

There are intermediate ethical positions as well, between outright refusal to accept a living donor organ and proactive solicitation of one. Some patients will not ask for a kidney but will accept one offered by someone they know. They draw the moral line at the place where unprompted, insistent generosity meets a request that could seem coercive because of the significance of the bond. Insistence and persistence on the part of the donor seems crucial to recipient judgments.

People who will accept an organ from a living person ultimately establish a hierarchy of potential donors, reflecting the construction of the ideal biosocial candidate for donation. For example: The son is running a business; he has four employees who rely on him. The daughter has two young children. But another daughter is not married, does not have children and does not have the financial responsibilities of the son. She is the ideal candidate. Or, the daughter with two children believes she is the most physically fit member of the family. She offers and is adamant about it. Or, the children have their lives ahead of them. I wouldn't accept from them because they may need their kidneys later on. But I will take a kidney from someone else, someone not as young as my children.

We often heard, at first, a negative injunction against asking one's spouse, children, siblings or other family to donate—"I'll never take an organ from one of my children." But the initial refusal to consider one's family member as a donor frequently gives way to acceptance in weeks or months because some patients feel extremely ill on dialysis and/or because they want the freedom and better health that a transplant promises: "I was getting sicker and she kept offering."

Thus the family (and friends, acquaintances and most recently, strangers) serve as the agent of medicine and its goals.[7]

> "The children talked me into it. I said, I'm not taking my daughter's kidney! But other family members persuaded me. I was hopeful that I could get a cadaver—right up to the night I was hospitalized. My point was, I didn't want to take an organ from my child. It didn't feel like it was the right thing to do. Help should go the other way, from parent to child. There were periods of time I just really didn't want to do it. I just went along with the flow. I was going along for the ride because things were being arranged for me."

Donors

Donors' and prospective donors' side of the story of obligation and gift-giving reflects their expectation that mortality can be, and should be, pushed back into the hazy future. Donors and prospective donors express a shared ethical clarity about their responsibility. From a daughter: "There was no choice, no decision-making. This was simply the thing to do—to donate a kidney. He needed one. I could save his life." From a friend: "I don't think of it as a great thing. I just think of it as a normal thing that people you know would do . . . I just think it's a

natural thing." Or, "We're full-blooded Greek;" "We're Italian/
Spanish;" "We're Dutch;" "We're Japanese-American;" "so you
stick by one another. Family is the most important thing, and
this was a matter of the family unit."

The nature of obligation—from generation to generation—
was perhaps expressed most clearly by a fifty-four-year old
woman who donated a kidney to her boss and friend, who, she
noted, was like family. Though she thought about the impact her
donation would have on her own daughter and her daughter's
children, she did not think about it for very long:

> ". . . He said that he had a kidney problem and that he
> was gonna look for a donor because he didn't want to be on
> dialysis. He gave me something to read, I think. But before
> then, I said yes . . . I've known X for a long, long time. We're
> like family—it wasn't a question. It was an easy decision. My
> daughter has one kidney. She had cancer when she was six
> years old and they took a kidney out. That was thirty years ago.
> So, I know a little bit about it. Knowing that no harm was going
> to come to me and knowing that, if down the line my daughter
> needed a kidney, she had some sort of back-up, I think that's
> what made it easy. I knew all of that. . . . I discussed it with
> my daughter and my son—what I was gonna do; how they felt
> about it. My daughter was totally for it and she and I talked
> about it and I didn't even have to say anything. She was the
> one who said, 'Well, I have two sons, you know, if I need a
> kidney . . .' And that made me even more comfortable."

This donor is not unique in assuming that the transfer of her
own kidney to another could instigate the 'natural' obligation of
younger generations to donate to older kin and like-kin in the
future. That always potential obligation of the body of others
does not appear troublesome.

The Shape of Freedom

Enacting one's own freedom—through one's right, obligation
and commitment to health and long life—is a complex and
demanding enterprise. Growing older without aging[8] is the form

that freedom takes in our era of routine life-extension, an era that might well be characterized by the merging of the "right to live" and "making live."[i] The case of kidney transplantation offers one empirical example of how that freedom is understood and organized in and by an aging society in which the biomedicalization of life is a dominant form of discursive power.

Death and "choice" about death are now thoroughly medicalized in the affluent sectors of the west, and the biopolitics of the "right to die" have been clearly (though narrowly) articulated in the last decades—control over the timing and means of death, symptom management, humane rather than heroic intervention. Subjectification vis-à-vis death is marked by the right, responsibility and freedom (if one is fortunate enough) to authorize the location, style and timing of one's own end.[j] By comparison, while life itself and the stages of life (including the fetal) are also thoroughly medicalized, the freedom to "make live" in late life opens up a new truth, about the relationship among intersubjectivity, obligation of and through the body, and the desire for extended life. The impacts of the mandate to live on the transformation of the subject are revealed in a more diffuse, less homogeneous fashion than are the impacts of the "right to die."

While genetic research and its clinical applications have and will continue to have obvious implications for the nature of the human, there are many clinical practices, not based on contemporary genetic research, that impact our relationship to life, its end and our responsibilities toward one another and that lie, it seems, under the radar of societal scrutiny. Routine kidney transplantation at older ages is simply one of them. Cardiac bypass surgery performed on persons over age ninety, tube-feeding of the profoundly demented and permanently comatose are others. If and when these interventions are publicly noticed it is not because the procedures themselves are thought to alter what is "natural" about the body, the self or the social, but rather because of disagreement among patient, family, physician, medical institution and/or the state over who has the right to authorize life or death—to let die and make live. (And we saw this very clearly in the case of Terri Schiavo.)

The desire and expectation for greater longevity, a given in affluent sectors of society that is driving a great deal of biomedical research and clinical intervention, is leading us to greater biologization of our moral commitments.

Notes

1. This article, presented at the conference by Sharon Kaufman and based on her ethnographic research, is part of a collaborative project among the three authors. The research on which it is based was funded by the National Institute on Aging, grant AG20962, to Sharon R. Kaufman, Principal Investigator. This article is an abridged version of Sharon R. Kaufman, Ann J. Russ, and Janet K. Shim, "Aged Bodies and Kinship Matters: The Ethical Field of Kidney Transplant," *American Ethnologist* 33:1 (2006): 81–99.

2. Dorry L. Segev et al., "Kidney Paired Donation and Optimizing the Use of Live Donor Organs," *Journal of the American Medical Association* 18 (2005): 471–476.

3. Zygmunt Bauman, *Mortality, Immortality and Other Life Strategies* (Stanford: Stanford University Press, 1992).

4. Marcel Mauss, *The Gift: Forms and Functions of Exchange in Archaic Societies*, trans. Ian Cunnison (New York: Norton, 1967).

5. Renee C. Fox and Judith P. Swazey, *Spare Parts: Organ Replacement in American Society* (New York: Oxford University Press, 1992). Renee C. Fox and Judith P. Swazey, *The Courage to Fail* (New Brunswick, NJ: Transaction Publishers, 2002).

6. Sarah Franklin, *Embodied Progress: A Cultural Account of Assisted Conception* (London: Routledge, 1997). David Schneider, *American Kinship: A Cultural Account*, 2nd edition (Chicago: University of Chicago Press, 1980). Marilyn Strathern, *Reproducing the Future* (New York, Routledge, 1992).

7. Joao Biehl, "Life of the Mind: The Interface of Psychopharmaceuticals, Domestic Economies, and Social Abandonment," *American Ethnologist* 31 (2004): 475–496.

8. Stephen Katz and Barbara Marshall, "New Sex for Old: Lifestyle, Consumerism, and the Ethics of Aging Well," *Journal of Aging Studies* 17 (2003): 3–16.

9. Paul Rabinow and Nikolas Rose, "Thoughts on the Concept of Biopower Today" (paper presented at the conference *Vital Politics*, London School of Economics and Political Science, London, UK, September 5–7, 2003).

10. Sharon R. Kaufman, . . . *And a Time to Die: How American Hospitals Shape the End of Life* (New York: Scribner, 2005).

16

Aging and Trans-aging

Helene Moglen

I remember the first time I understood that my body was genuinely going to betray me—not with small injuries to vanity, or customary failures of agility, or lapses of physical discipline, for which compensation always seems possible. This form of betrayal was determined, inevitable, and irreversible. It exposed the fissures between inner and outer, the psychic and the material, the familiar and the strange. For me, it signaled simultaneously the erasure and the certainty of generational difference.

The shock of recognition was provoked—in my fortieth year—by my image in the mirror. The face prepared for self-reflection—eyes and mouth faintly smiling. Pale skin and blonde hair enhanced by the black line of a high-necked sweater: a line miraculously interrupted by a fold of flesh. I shifted the angle of reflection, the lighting, the pose. Nothing changed. Nothing restored the clear curve of the chin or the sharp edge of the sweater. Genetic revenge. My mother was beautiful until she died at eighty-six, but when she turned forty, her neck started to collapse. For years, her face was a flower on a crumpled stem. Not usually confiding, she told me once that men and women clutched their necks when they looked at her, fearful of a contagious transformation in themselves. Here was the mortal disease of aging—and I had caught it.

Of course, seeing one's own reflection in the mirror inevitably produces an experience of the uncanny, which is central, as Lacan has taught us, to the process of becoming human subjects. In our reflections, we glimpse the familiar self we have prepared ourselves to see and a shadow self, which is alien and unknown. We attribute psychic interiority and depth to the familiar image and perceive its unfamiliar double as a false self in which true identity is clothed. Usually, we are able to submerge the strange in the recognized reflection, maintaining an illusion of psychic coherence and integrity. But sometimes the relation of inner and outer, strange and familiar, is reversed. Then the surface image is perceived as an unfamiliar version of the hidden self, which is experienced as oddly "real." Fantasies of integration are subverted in such moments. The real self is trapped inside an unreal body: a woman inhabiting the trappings of a man, for example, or a young person imprisoned in an old. The wrinkled face, the indistinctness of the chin, the oddly crumpled neck: these are marks of an impostor who betrays the being she impersonates.

One might respond to such epiphanal experiences by wishing to replace the visible but unfamiliar self with an embodied version of the internal image—an image that is produced by memory, by a desiring imagination, or by some uneasy combination of the two. But the effort to literalize this shadowy presence—through pharmaceutical and surgical interventions, for example—only maintains it, frozen, in the self. When one is obsessed with the ghostly figure of loss, one *becomes* the lost object, closed—in the present—to enlivening connection and dynamic change. Living out the narrative of the incorporated other entails a melancholic regression: psychic bondage to a fantasized identity or to an unrealized, and unrealizable, ideal.

This melancholic psychic structure is elaborated in familiar stories of the double. Robert Louis Stevenson created one version in *Dr. Jekyll and Mr. Hyde,* for example, while Oscar Wilde produced another in *The Portrait of Dorian Gray.* Both fictions suggest how the banished other (perverse desire or decadent old age) continues to threaten the ideal self with its return, offering forms of knowledge and states of being that have already been refused. In these melancholic fictions, the transformed self can never become whole but is always marked by the excess of its rejected shadow, which erupts into consciousness from its sepulcher in the unconscious.

Although the melancholic response to dissonant experiences of aging is inexhaustibly self-referential, its determinants are social. Cultural biases function, as we know, through oppositional constructions. They establish the attractiveness of bodies and their antitheses, which inspire revulsion, anxiety and fear. Our memories of earlier incarnations are filtered through cultural representations that intensify desires for altered physical states. Society obligingly produces, commodifies and markets the knowledge and technology that make such bodily transformations possible.

Of course, there are different ways of conceptualizing and responding to shocking encounters with an aging self. It is true that psychic fragmentation is inevitably disconcerting—but it is also comfortingly familiar. Aging is not the achievement of a moment, after all. It takes place across a lifetime that begins with conception and ends with death. It is a multiple, ambiguous and contradictory process, which provides us— continuously and simultaneously—with images of past, present, lost, embodied and imagined selves. In shifting configurations, these images comprise the discontinuous yet persistent thread of our identities, which are not integrated, which are not merely split, and which can neither be reduced to nor separated from the limitations and requirements of the body.

If we approach the aging process in a spirit not of melancholia but of mourning, we can accept the self that surfaces in moments of conscious reflection as an accretion and layering of innumerable selves: a compilation that is subject to endless, subterranean revision. Former moods, affects, thoughts and states of being, which are embedded in personal history, are never completely erased but remain psychically available for elaboration and conversion. So, the omnivorously desiring infant inhabits the body of the lover. The grandmother who plays peek-a-boo with the baby rediscovers her own infantile delight. The scholar's research is catalyzed by the tantalized voyeurism of the child.

Adopting the mourner's position does not require a denial of profound losses we suffer as we age: losses of relationships, ideals, capacities, and opportunities. But it does help us see the dangers we face when we tether ourselves to an obsessive desire for their reincarnation. Mourning allows us to move beyond the knowledge of whom or what we have lost, as Freud urges us to do, so that we can understand what we have lost in our loved objects and ideals: what we have lost, therefore, in ourselves. When we mourn the loss of our youthful bodies, we are grieving for the contexts in which they were formed, for the states of mind that gave them meaning, for the significance they achieved through their interactions with the expressive worlds of other bodies. This form of mourning changes our understanding of the relation of consciousness and time. To remain mired in the past is to deny the alluring mystery of present and future. That allure persists until the body does finally overwhelm the mind— during exceptional illness, for example, or in cases of "deep age," and approaching death—when loss becomes irreparable. Then the horizon flattens and dimensionality disappears.

In order to distinguish this dynamic version of aging from its melancholic alternative, we might describe it in terms of "trans-aging" —emphasizing the constant, erratic movement that takes place in consciousness across, between and among the endlessly overlapping stages of life. This renaming is intended to evoke a comparison with other conceptual and experiential efforts of category crossing, particularly those that pertain to sex and gender, which are similarly defined by the interrelation of body, mind and culture. The discourse of trans-aging is located conceptually between the discourse of trans-sexuality and the discourse of trans-gender. Like transgender theory and practice, it resists categorical identities, along with the power relations and psychological rigidity that such identities entail. But while trans-aging emphasizes the cultural construction of developmental stages, it also insists upon the relentless materiality of bodies. It is this refusal to collapse the physical into the cultural body that trans-aging and trans-sexuality fundamentally share.

Indeed, it is precisely because transsexual narratives have recorded social, psychological and physical journeys from one specifically sexed body to another that trans-sexuality has been widely understood as a transitional phase. But, as Jay Prosser points out in Second Skins: The Body Narratives of Transexuality, there is a growing movement among transsexuals to maintain their bodies in an in-between state, refusing a specific destination at the transition's end.[1] This re-conceptualization of the transsexual journey as open ended and neither/nor represents a strategic effort to sustain ambiguity and ambivalence, aligning—but not merging—transsexual with transgender identities. The body continues to signify, but it signifies, in a sense, paradoxically.

This version of trans-sexuality provides a useful (if partial) model for a discourse of trans-aging. It is rooted in an acknowledgement of the social, psychological and, above all, physical meanings of difference, and it affirms a theory and practice that values creativity, multiplicity, and subversion. The adoption of such a trans-sexual practice is the result of conscious choice, as Prosser makes clear: a commitment to alternative perspectives in the face of social stereotypes, psychic pressures and the irreducible materiality of bodies. It requires the shaping of personal narratives that, in their specificities, interrogate and challenge dominant cultural scripts.

Narratives of the self are crucial also to psychic and cultural constructions of those who refuse identification with a concept of aging that focuses only on lack and loss but who still acknowledge the vicissitudes of the aging body. When the outside is categorically classified and socially dismissed, the nature of interiority tends to be assumed. Social fictions of aging reflect both the need to create difference, by projecting that which is feared onto "aged" others, and the dread of difference, which threatens the solidity of boundaries and illusions of control. Shaped by ageism, in its myriad public and private forms, such fictions produce self-hatred on one side, and social discrimination on the other.

Personal narratives of trans-aging are produced from a place not of the other, not even of the self. They articulate the interrelated consciousnesses of many selves, which are of many ages and of no age at all. Not fixated on the literal specificities of bodies, they explore the intriguing meanings of embodiment, with its erasure of barriers between inside and out. To the extent that personal narratives emerge from dynamic intra- and inter-psychic processes, they resist paralytic melancholia. To the extent that they enable self-recognition and self-creation, they transcend the alienated relations of mirroring. Articulating while helping to shape multifaceted subjectivities, they explode the flattened, stereotypical projections of others.

When I was forty, I was panicked by my reflection in the mirror: panicked by the emergence of my own aging double, which was also a ghostly image of my mother. By the time I was fifty, I had accepted the fact of that doubleness with qualified humor—and attempted to approach it inventively. Despite the fact that I had always viewed the practice as barbaric, I pierced my ears—as a visual distraction. It was an effort to redirect my own gaze in order to diminish the power of the specter. The strategy was, in many ways, successful, although it required an extensive collection of earrings to support it.

In the years that followed, external events colluded to create and resurrect a confusion of identities that were molded by profound loss and by extraordinary possibilities. Who I was, who I was becoming, who—eventually—I would be; none of this could be discovered in the mirror, which became increasingly irrelevant to my research. Even as the years have written themselves with increasing indelibility on my body, the meanings of their markings have multiplied in their ambiguity and contradiction. One narrative—one effort of self-telling and self-making—is inadequate to contain them. Each represents a stage of the crossing, a moment in the transition, a layer of the palimpsest. Each is, like aging itself, painfully truncated and astonishingly full.

Note

1. Jay Prosser, *Second Skins: The Body Narratives of Transexuality,* New York: Columbia University Press, 1998, p. 11.

17

A Note of a Sportswriter's Daughter: Companion Species

Donna Haraway

November 3, 1981

Dear Dad,

Your retirement from the Denver *Post* has been present to me for weeks now. I want to write to you about what your work has meant to me since I was a small girl. I tell all the people who are important to me, "My father is a sportswriter. He loves his work. He is good at it, and he passed on to me the center of my feeling about work as a way of living at least as much as making a living." Your pleasure in words has been central to your work. I saw you *enjoy* words. You showed your children words as tools to sculpt fuller lives. I read your stories for years, and I learned a daily, reliable craft to tell important stories. Your work taught me that "writing a story" is a very fine way to "make a living." I saw you consistently insist on writing about the parts of people you could affirm, not because you hid sordid things, but because you allowed people their beauty. I think that is why you loved the game story best. I saw you chronicle dramas, rituals, feats, skills, mindful bodies in motion. In sports writing, you penned stories that made living bigger, expansive, generous.

I remember going to the old Denver Bears Stadium in the 1950s when Bill and the other boys were bat and ball boys. I regretted not being able to *be* a bat boy in the same way I regretted not being able to *be* a Jesuit, so that I heard my dolls' confessions in my closet with the sliding doors and said mass for them on my dresser. I have changed since then from a junior Catholic theologian to a much less innocent feminist scribbler, from a parochial school basketball forward, to a writer of her own game stories. You gave me the same skills you gave my brothers, Bill and Rick. You taught us all to score about the same time we learned to read.[1] That night in 1958 when you and the *Rocky Mountain News* scribe Chet Nelson asked me how I had scored a contested baseball play on which you couldn't agree, and then used my scoring, gave me something precious: you recognized me in your work. You gave me your regard.

My father was a sportswriter.

With love,
Donna

Bodies in the making, indeed. This essay is a note of a sportswriter's daughter. It is writing that I must do, because it's about a legacy, an inheritance in the flesh. To come to accept the body's unmaking, I need to re-member its becoming. I need to recognize all the members, animate and inanimate, that make up the knot of a particular life, my father Frank Outten Haraway's life.

My husband Rusten and I have been privileged to accompany our aging parents in the last months and years of their lives. On September 29, 2005, my brothers and I held my father while he died, alert and present, in our hands. We held him during the process of his no longer being there. This was not a process uniquely of his no longer being present as a soul, or a mind, or a person, or an interior, or a subject. No, as his body cooled, his *body* was no longer there. The corpse is not the body. Rather, the body is always in the making; it is always a vital entanglement of heterogeneous scales, times, and kinds of beings webbed into fleshly presence, always a becoming, always constituted in relating. The corpse's consignment to the earth as ashes is, I think, a recognition that, in death, it is not simply the person or the soul who goes. That knotted thing we call the body has left; it is undone. My father is undone, and that is why I must re-member him. I and all those who lived entangled with him become his flesh; we are kin to the dead because their bodies have touched us. The body of my father is the body that I knew as his daughter. I inherit in the flesh, in material troping, tripping, that joins text and body in what I call material semiosis and semiotic materiality.

Mine is a looping set of stories of the generations; my story is about inheriting the craft of writing looping, braided stories, stories of the game. Born in 1916, my father was a sportswriter for the Denver *Post* for forty-four years. After retiring from the paper in 1981, he continued to work in the Denver sports world, as the baseball official scorer for the National League for the Colorado Rockies, and as part of the statistics crews for Denver Nuggets basketball and Broncos football. His last working game was in September, 2004, when he was eighty-seven years old. Writing his own epitaph, he lived and died as a sportswriter, or as he put it, as a fan who got paid to do what he loved.

I try to be something of a sports woman; we will come back to that. In the university, I too am paid to do what I love. In this essay, I write about the inheritance of being a journalist's daughter, a sportswriter's daughter, about my effort to gain the father's regard, to gain his approval, to somehow have his writing be about my sport, my game. I write out of a child's need in order to honor an ongoing adult love.

I'm a heterosexual daughter, more or less, of a relentlessly heterosexual father, a girl child who never had her father's heterosexual gaze. His was a deliberate withholding of the gaze of potential incest, I now think. I both loathed and envied his gender-conventional sexualization of other women and girls. My husband's sister Suze and I talk together about our fathers, who could not look at their daughters as beautiful physically because they dared not. But I got my father's regard in another, life-giving, bodily way—I got his respect. This is a different specular economy of generational passage, no less corporeal and no less full of desire and lure, no less leery of the law, no less in the game, but in an economy that leads the daughter to remember in joy and grief. This kind of look has made my body what it is in life as a writer and as a woman playing a sport. I want to take us, take me, through part of this legacy.

Consider "regard" and "respect" a bit longer. I am drawn by the tones of this kind of active looking at/regard (both as verb, *respecere*, and as *respectus*) that I sought and experienced with and from my father.[2] The specific relationality in this kind of regard holds my attention: to have regard to, to see differently, to esteem, to look back, to hold in regard, to hold in seeing, to be touched by another's regard, to heed, to take care of. This kind of regard aims to release and be released in oxymoronic, necessary, autonomy-in-relation. Autonomy as the fruit of and inside relation. Autonomy as trans-acting. Quite the opposite of the gaze/look usually studied in cultural theory! And certainly not the fruit of the gaze of incest.

In recent speaking and writing on "companion species," I have been trying to live inside the many tones of regard/respect/seeing each other/looking back at/meeting/optic-haptic encounter. Species and respect are in optic/haptic/affective/cognitive touch—they are at table together, they are messmates, companions, in company, *cum panis*. I also love the inherent oxymoron of "species"—always both logical type and relentlessly particular, always tied to *specere* and yearning/looking toward *respecere*. "Species" includes animal and human as categories, and much more besides; and we would be ill advised to assume which categories are in play and shaping each other in flesh and logic in constitutive encounterings.

In all those senses, I see the regard I am trying to think and feel as part of something not proper to either humanism or posthumanism. "Companion species"—co-shapings all the way down, in all sorts of temporalities and corporealities—is my awkward term for a not-humanism in which species of all sorts are in question. For me, even when we speak only of people, the animal/human/living/nonliving category separations fray inside the kind of encountering worthy of regard. The ethical regard that I am trying to speak and write can be experienced across many sorts of species differences.[3] The lovely part is that we can only know by looking, and looking back. *Respecere.*

For the last few years, I have been writing under the sign of companion species, perhaps partly to tweak my colleagues' sense of proper species behavior. They have been remarkably patient; indeed, they get it that "companion species" does not mean smallish animals treated like indulged children-in-fur-coats (or fins or feathers) in late imperial societies. Companion species is a permanently undecidable category, a category-in-question that insists on the relation as the smallest unit of being and of analysis. By species I mean, with thanks to Karen Barad's theory of agential realism and intra-action, a kind of intra-ontics/intra-antics that does not predetermine the status of the species as artifact, machine, landscape, organism, or human being.[4] Singular and plural, species resonate with the tones of logical types, of the relentlessly specific, of coin and metal money, of the real presence in the Catholic Eucharist, of Darwinian kinds, of SF aliens, and of much else. Species, like the body, are internally oxymoronic, full of their own others, full of messmates, of companions.

Every species is a multispecies crowd. Human exceptionalism is what companion species cannot abide. In the face of companion species, human exceptionalism shows itself to be the specter that damns the body to illusion, to reproduction of the same, to incest, and so makes re-membering impossible. Under the material-semiotic sign of companion species, I am interested in the ontics and antics of significant otherness, in the ongoing making of the partners through the making itself, in the making of bodied lives in the game. Partners do not preexist their relating; the partners are precisely what come out of the inter/intra-relating of fleshly, significant, semiotic-material being. This is the ontological choreography that Charis Thompson writes about.[5] I'm telling a looping story of figuration, of ontics, of bodies in the making, of play in which all the messmates are not human.

Indeed, perhaps this is the daughter's knowledge, which is made possible by the kind of regard/respect her father gave— the knowledge that we have never been human and so are not caught in that cyclopean trap of mind and matter, action and passion, actor and instrument. Because we have never been the philosopher's human, we are bodies in braided, ontic, and antic relatings.

And so, we write the game story. In this account, the messmates with my father—the constitutive companion species knots that get my attention—are not myself nor any other organism, but a pair of crutches and two wheelchairs. These were his partners in the game of living well.

When he was sixteen months old, my father fell and injured his hip. Tuberculosis set in. It subsided, only to return with a vengeance in 1921 when he slipped on an oiled floor. Tuberculosis lodged in the upper leg, knee, and hip bones, in a period when there was no treatment. We get this version of the history of the body from a tenth-grade school assignment, "The Autobiography of Frank Haraway," that we found after Dad's death in his orderly, but still packrat-inspired, files.[6] His own father had moved to Colorado Springs from Tennessee and Mississippi (the state line actually ran through the family house) in order to heal from pulmonary tuberculosis in a Rocky Mountain spa town that makes me recall *Magic Mountain*. My father's childhood tuberculosis meant that from an early age he could not move without excruciating pain. He spent the ages of eight to about eleven in bed in a full-length body cast from his chest to his knees, not able to attend school and so learning with a private tutor. Not expected to live, nonetheless, eventually he healed. But the hip joints were permanently calcified, and he was left rigid with no plane of motion, no ability to bend, from the hips. He could not separate his legs in any direction. (This fact made me curious in my adolescent years about how my parents pulled off

Frank and his younger brother Jack Haraway
playing neighborhood baseball around 1930

feats of conception—ordinary epistemophilia, with a twist. There was more than a little joking in our house about these matters.)

My father's father had money until a few years into the Depression. My grandfather was a sports promoter as well as the owner of Piggly Wiggly grocery stores in Colorado. A business man and community figure, he brought sports figures to Denver like Babe Ruth and Lou Gehrig, who came to Dad's house and signed a baseball for him while he was still confined to bed. My grandfather and his industrialist colleagues founded the white men's basketball leagues that preceded professional basketball as we now know it. The players for B. F. Goodrich, Akron Goodyear, Piggly Wiggly, and other Midwestern and Western industrial basketball teams were all white men destined to be middle-level managers. The bodily practices of racialization come in many forms, not least the braiding of family, sports, and business. My father was a sportswriter; that is part of how I am white; it is part of the game story. Race and money are part of how my father became a sportswriter.

My grandfather got Dad a wheelchair as soon as he was able to get out of his bed and body cast, so he could go to the old Merchant's Park and watch the ballgames. But he was not just a spectator. From his wheelchair, in his typical semi-recumbent seated posture dictated by his unaccommodating hips, Dad played baseball in the neighborhood. I have a picture of him and his younger brother Jack, about twelve and thirteen years old, both wearing characteristic pajama-mimic baseball pants, clutching bottles of Coke. Dad is in his wheelchair, flashing his trademark, gap-toothed smile that showed up years later on the sports page cartoons drawn by Bob Bowie at the beginning of baseball spring training. Another photo shows my pimply-faced father swinging the bat with rather elegant athletic form. Dad was known in the neighborhood, I am told, as a good player, or at least a popular one. That wheelchair was in a companion-species relation to the boy; the whole body was organic flesh as well as wood and metal; the player was on wheels, grinning. Yet, perhaps not always grinning. At the end of a neighborhood game, so the family story goes, when their ancient baseball fell apart definitively and for the last time, the other kids persuaded Dad to bring out his Babe Ruth–Lou Gehrig autographed treasure. Sure, Dad thought, we only have one out to go. Dad watched the batter hit the ball past the fielder's outstretched glove. The ball rolled down the urban gutter into the sewers, where it continues to fertilize narratives of loss and nostalgia— and narratives of the dramatic plays in a game.

When he graduated from Randall, the private high school he attended in his wheel chair, Dad got his crutches and galloped off to Denver University, where he became student sports editor of the DU *Clarion*. His track career at DU was cut short after an unauthorized race with a broken-legged football player, who was temporarily locomoting with crutches, that was set up by the other athletes on the track around the football field, starting gun and all. Dad's trusty cherry-wood crutches under his armpits, swinging in long arcs, my father won the race handily; but his opponent fell and broke his other leg, prompting the coach to warn Dad off of any further competitive exploits. These crutches belong corporeally in a life built out of relational, enabling objectifications, of coming into being through meldings with the physicality of the wheelchair, the bed, the cast, the crutches, all of which produced a vital, living, achieving sportswriter.

Aided by his crutches, Dad developed a sense of balance that sustained him without the "sticks," as he called them, while standing and taking tiny steps using his partially flexible knees. That way, with unreturnable serves—in later years, mostly made illegal—and enviable timing, he won three straight Colorado State Table Tennis Championships in the 1930s. If you've ever watched table tennis, you know it's a sport that requires covering a lot of ground with your legs, which was exactly what my father could not do. He won because of hand-eye coordination, balance, guts, upper-body strength, mind/body inventiveness, and desire—and because of his living in relationship to his own physicality in a way that never for a minute considered either denial or immobility—i.e., living outside the body—as a viable option.

To be in companion species relationship was the viable way of life. He was lucky to have a concatenated series of partners, including the wheelchair, the crutches, and the attention and resources of his parents and friends. The vitality came from living with regard to all those partners. Another photo that spilled out of Dad's files, one we put near his casket at the mortuary, eloquently makes this point. The photographer caught Dad unawares from behind in the late afternoon during batting practice before the game. Dad is in third-base coaching box looking toward the pitcher's mound. It's hard to be sure, but he looks to be about forty years old, and he's wearing a his typical checkered sports shirt. At first, it just seems he's standing relaxed on slightly-A-frame-positioned crutches. Then you see that he has his knees bent at a ninety-degree angle, with the soles of his shoes pointed to the camera. He is standing relaxed on his crutches all right, still and calm and utterly airborne.

My father lived his adult life, with his crutches, at speed. What I remember as a little girl was running down the block to keep up, not walking with someone less abled. Still, I need to return to walking for a while to understand better how modifying bodies work. Early on, I noticed that my two brothers, both my older brother Bill and my younger brother Rick, neither of whom had hip disorders of any kind, walked a lot like my father. They still do, if you know what to look for. They literally embodied the gait of this man. This fact was not much remarked in the family; after all, it was normal for sons to be like their father, wasn't it? Theirs was a mimetic looping through the storied, masculine bodies of fathers and sons, which at no point was regarded as mimicking disability, or any sort of oddity. The term "disability" didn't enter the family, not because there was denial about the need for crutches, but because these objects were normal parts of paternal equipment, all meanings intended. Certainly, they were part of the reproductive apparatus that shaped the bodies of my brothers.

This shared gait was about coming into cognizance of, in regard to, our father's body in a life-shaping way. In a sense, Dad's crutches symbiotically infused the bodies of all the family. My brothers and I would, naturally, borrow his crutches to try them out and see how fast we could go. We all did things like that, but only my brothers literally walked my father's walk. I did not have my father's gait; I had his way with language. My brothers did too, actually—Bill, as a financial adviser, in the idiom and lineage of our businessman grandfather; and Rick, as a social worker and peace and justice worker, in the vulgate of our mother, Dorothy Maguire's Catholic formation, where what later came to be called the "preference for the poor" was both doctrine and life-affirming bread. Trembling when she had to give her much-practiced treasurer's reports to the PTA, Mom shunned verbal public performance; but she knew the word was made flesh in taking people's needs and pain to her own heart. Laughing, she and I played with Latin words, when I pestered her with my worries that it might be a sin to use sacred language in an overly serious, speculative child's fantasies. She was eloquent with good advice for me, even though I knew her own mind/body, in the vise-grip of belief, was blasted by the mine-fields of Catholic contradiction and unspeakable yearning in the teeth of doctrine. She had the more speculative, self-analytical consciousness in our family, but not the tools for expression. In 1960 she died of a heart attack, on a Monday morning in October after we had all left for school and work. I think my father never had any idea about her entrapment, but he did know her gift. I also think the physicality through which I came into relationship with my father, through which I got his regard, was through the sensuality of words and the acts of writing. We talked about, punned on, played with, and ate words for dinner; they were our food too, even while we ate from my mother's mind/body, in her cooking and in her loneliness and barely acknowledged physical vulnerability.

In his eighties, Dad needed his crutches more and more for getting around, even in the house. Then, he started falling. He fell hard in January, 2005, and broke his hip. Because of the extensive scarifying calcification from the childhood tuberculosis, there was no way to use a pin, or an external stabilization device, or anything else to hold the separated bones together well enough so they could heal well enough to give him half a chance to walk or even stand again. So, out of bed for decades, he lived his last eight months mostly back in bed, again in poorly relieved pain, relearning how to be mobile without legs. His bone-deep regard for people did not fail him. He flirted mercilessly with the nurses, Claudia and Lori, and the massage therapist. Tracy, with the same cheerful heterosexual self-confidence that plagued my feminist soul and roused my latent envy. He also formed gentle, trusting bonds with male caretakers—John, the blond Denver kid, and Lucky, the immigrant from Ghana—unaided by the specular and verbal devices of flirtation and across gulfs of race, class, and intimate bodily dependency. I thought the women who cared for him became his friends in spite of, not because of, his flirting; they knew that another kind of regard was operating even more powerfully, if less articulately. They still call my family, the men and the women call, to see how we are doing.

In the last months, Dad got a talented cyborg wheelchair that was radically different from the 1920s chariot I see in the old photos. The ad brochure promised everything but flight. Dad developed an affectionate, joking relationship with Drew, the kind and able wheelchair salesman. The physical therapist, Shawna, set up orange traffic cones in a line for him in the hallway of the rehab center, the one we called Rocky Road, so that he could practice navigating without taking down fellow dubiously ambulatory residents. It didn't take us long to up the limits on his liability insurance. Semi-recumbent, he had to pass Shawna's driving test with this chip-implanted, over-achieving chair, which he never for a minute trusted, but of which he was rather proud, even though he couldn't get into it and out of it on his own. This chair never quite became a beloved significant other. This partner was overwhelmingly about loss from which there would be no exit. It was a much fancier chair than the one of his youth, but it no longer signified getting well and going to the games. This chair, this transaction between wary companion species, was about the practice of dying. Even so, the chair assisted this process with companions of many species, both the apparatuses and the people, in a way that continued to stimulate a sportswriter's eye for the vitality of movement in the world.

The apparatus of companion species included satellite installations and a new television set to watch the games and phone calls and visits with friends and colleagues to continue his professional relationship with, and life-long pleasure in, sports. Brother Rick and his wife Roberta even got him in a van and to a baseball game once, to the National League press box named for him; but it was too hard, too painful, to do again. His partners of many species included all the means that he and we could imagine for staying in the game as long as he could.

And then he couldn't. He got pneumonia, and decided not to treat it. He decided to go, because he judged that in any meaningful sense, he could stay in the game no longer. His game story was filed. Indeed, on his desk we found a stickie with the logo of the "morning fish wrapper," i.e., the *Rocky Mountain News*, the rival newspaper, stuck in a plastic paperweight cube, on which he had penciled his last game story for us to savor: "When the good Lord decides I can no longer go to the games I love so much, I just want to be remembered as a happy man who loved his family, who loved people, and as a sports fan who got paid for writing what he saw." We worried for a while that we should have cremated his crutches with his remains; they belonged together; they were one vital body; both should go. Instead, Rick took the crutches home and put them in his living room, where they link us all to our ancestors, those companion species in other kinds of ontic and antic time.

My father was not a particularly self-reflective person; he didn't theorize these matters. As far as I could tell—and to my shame, I never tired of trying to recast him into the mold I wanted him to fit, from praying for his conversion to Catholicism when I was little to trying to get him to read books and analyze everything under the sun when I was older—he didn't reflect on these ramifying mimeses, these looping stories of body/minds coming to presence in the world through engaging companion species. I think that his relationship to his work and to his life was to write the game stories, and to be *in* the game. He never wanted to be a columnist or run the sports department of a big city newspaper. He certainly never wanted to tell the stories about the commercial, social, and political apparatus that makes professional sports possible. He was not reflective about what it might mean for a man with rigid hips to spend a good part of his adult life whacking the bums of football players in locker rooms, though my first husband earnestly asked him about that more than once. Jaye was gay and extremely interested in homosocial physicality of both sexual and nonsexual kinds. He kept trying to get Dad to think about what the hell was going on, and to think through his own multiple bodily relationships with men. These were not Dad's ways of being. These were his children's problems and tasks. He was a man who wrote the game story, and stayed in the game, and whose regard as a father I have not stopped needing.

Because of that need, in respect and with regard to all the players, I end this story, which has taken us through beds, casts, wheelchairs, crutches, and back to chairs, with another game story. As a woman in her fifties, I started playing a demanding sport with a member of another species a few years ago—with a dog, the dog of my heart, Cayenne, a Klingon Warrior Princess who was bred to be a working Australian Shepherd. Her speed and athletic talent are off the scales; but her partner, if eager and fit, is all too weighed down with modest talent and immoderate years. The sport is called agility, a game made up of twenty or so obstacles on a 100′ × 100′ course, in patterns set out by a diabolical judge, who evaluates the dog-human teams for speed and accuracy of performance.

Playing that sport with Cayenne, now—after thousands of hours of joint work and play—at the masters level, I recognize the looping ontics and antics, the partnerships-in-the-making that transform the bodies of the players in the doing itself. Agility is a team sport; both players make each other up in the flesh. Their principal task is to learn to be in the same game, to learn to see each other, to move as someone new that neither can be alone. To do that with a member of another biological species is not the same thing as doing it with a cheating, language-wielding, hominid partner. Cayenne and I must communicate throughout our being; and language in the orthodox linguist's sense is mostly in the way. The highs Cayenne and I experience come from focused, trained, responsive, joint movement at speed—from coursing together in mind/body through the patterns for the whole time, when the times in question range from twenty-five to fifty seconds, depending on the game. Speed alone is not enough; unfocused by each other's transforming regard, speed is chaos for us both. You can tell by all the penalties the judge assesses. The intensity that we both love is finely differentiated from the panic that destroys us. The "zone" for us is about speed, for sure, but speed organically braided in a joint, subject-transforming dance that makes the really good runs "slow"—i.e., we see and feel each other, see each other's eyes, feel each other's moving bodies. Not a wild dash, but trained regard.

From the time we started training for agility competition, true to my reforming zeal, I tried to convince my aged father—even after he broke his hip, he got no pass—what this sport is. It's not baseball, basketball, or football; it's not boxing, hockey, tennis, or golf. It's not even dog or horse racing. All of those he had had to write about at least once for a living; all of those were legible to a man of his generation, race, and class. No, I insisted, this time you learn agility, the sport of middle-aged women and their talented dogs, which will some day occupy the prime-time Monday-night TV slot, which is now making do with that man-breaking sport called football. I showed him diagrams of international-level masters' courses, explained what's involved technically, played videos of the USDAA Nationals when he was wild with pain and hallucinating on opiates, and wrote him accounts of Cayenne's and my variously comic or tragic exploits. He could not die; he was a sportswriter; he was my father. I wanted his regard; I wanted his approval; I wanted him to get it. I did not think he was watching or listening, except to murmur cheerful encouragement in a paternal tone, along the lines of "it's nice to have something you enjoy so much." This sport was off the radar for a sportswriter of his formation.

Then, last summer, when he was out of the rehab center, into his own room in an enhanced-care residential facility, and beginning to experience a lot less pain, just for fun I sent him a video of Cayenne and me running some courses at an AKC trial. I said, "This is what we did last weekend; this is what a bunch of the other players did; this is what the game looks like." He wrote me back a game story, crafted with all of his considerable professional skill.[7] He analyzed the runs; he took apart the coherencies and incoherencies. He saw in detail what was at stake, how the canine and human players moved, what worked and did not work. He wrote the game story as if he were a scout for a major league baseball team. He not only got it, he got it at the same professional level that he got the events that he was paid for, and he wrote it to me and Cayenne. He gave me—gave us—his regard. It's how he made a living.

Two Codas: Grief, Memory, and Story

I.

August 25, 2004

Dear Donnie,

Amazing! That was my first reaction upon seeing my (almost) sixty-year-old daughter running with her young, high-spirited, lightning-fast pooch in highly skilled competition. I marveled at the split-second timing required for you and Cayenne to communicate with each other. Yes, I noticed an occasional brief breakdown, quickly remedied as you resumed your run. Honestly, I was impressed. Little did I know when you cuddled up in my arms as a toddler that you would be running a dog in competition at the age of sixty! I replayed the video several times and thoroughly enjoyed it.

The die is cast. I am working on the Broncos' stats crew Friday night. Wish me luck.

Much love,

Dad

————————✦————————

That game was the last one Dad worked. He died a year later.

When I wrote "Note of a Sportswriter's Daughter: Companion Species," I remembered this letter as if it had been written in August 2005, not 2004. I remembered more detail on the runs than there was. Only after finishing the paper did I dig the letter out of my files to add quotes from Dad and get the dates for a footnote. Then I understood more than I wanted to know about how grief reworks truth to tell another truth. Fiercely accurate, I remembered the love in this letter. But I redid time, and time chastened me. The line between fiction and fact in family stories goes through the living room. The documenting practices of scholarship slice the heart, but they cannot undo the story. "Bodies in the Making: Transgressions and Transformations"— that is what stories chronicle. Stories re-member.

II.

After the Game:

"Somewhere Off 34th Street"

Filed by a sportswriter's daughter, December 11, 2005

In the season of recalling miracles on 34th Street, Kris Kringle must take a back seat to a marvel that happened closer to home. It happened to me and Cayenne in California's decidedly non-metropolitan Central Valley. Such a marvel will never happen again. Maybe I dreamed it. I hesitate to tell you in case I wake up. Maybe I'll write again later. No, I must check to see if reality holds. Here goes . . .

Cayenne and I got four perfect Qualifying Scores out of four runs (ExB Std, ExA JWW) at the Sacramento Dog Training Club's AKC trial at Rancho Murieta Friday and Saturday.

There, I said it. The sun is still shining, and so I'll risk telling you the rest. If the earth shakes, I'll stop.

Only international competitor Sharon Freilich's Rip, among all the Excellent class dogs of both A and B sections, was faster than us in three of the runs. In the "Jumpers with Weaves" run on Saturday, we were less than 0.5 seconds behind Sharon and Rip. Oh my. Now I will wake up for sure.

Recklessly, I forge on.

In the remaining run, an ExB Standard, we were fifth, behind a bunch of scruffy big name Border Collies, including both of Sharon's dogs (Rip and Cirque). Three seconds separated the second-to-fifth place dogs. If Cayenne had not wanted to discuss the latest scandal of the Bush administration while I was earnestly suggesting a down on the pause table, we might have been first and definitely second. So, we got two first places in our ExA JWW and a second in our other ExB Standard (behind Rip, or did I already mention that?), all with tight turns, serious focus, weaves to use in a teaching video, and blazing times. (I will not mention, although perhaps this is the reason the sun is still shining and the earth not shaking, our less-than-perfect start line holds.)

Am I happy? Is Cayenne a Klingon Warrior Princess? Oh yes. How do I know? Because the sun is still shining.

Notes

1. Two of my older brother's children, Mark and Debra, learned Dad's scoring system. Mark said that, across the gulfs of a continent and their own parents' divorce, this way of scoring bound them to a grandfather they barely knew. To be literate in my family means knowing how to code the plays so that a game can be reconstructed in dramatic detail years later. Katie King, *Speaking with Things: An Introduction to Writing Technologies* (under review) teaches me how writing technologies make persons. See www.womensstudies.umd.edu/wmstfac/kking.

2. My reflections on "regard" are in conversation with Wlad Godzich, whose December 20, 2005, email response to my talk at the Bodies in the Making conference were both moving and helpful.

3. See Donna Haraway, *The Companion Species Manifesto: Dogs, People and Significant Otherness* (Chicago, Prickly Paradigm Press, 2003); Anna Tsing, "Unruly Edges: Mushrooms as Companion Species," in ms, 2004; Vinciane Despret, "The Body We Care For: Figures of Anthropo-zoo-genesis," *Body and Society* 10, no. 2 (2004): 111-34. For the join of optics and haptics in species encounters, see Eva Shawn Hayward, "Jellyfish Optics: Immersion in Marine TechnoEcology," Meetings of the Society for Literature and Science, Durham, NC, October, 2004.

4. Karen Barad, "Invertebrate Visions: Diffractions, Mutations, Re(con)figurations, and the Ethics of Mattering," in ms., 2004 (based on chapter 8 from Barad's book-in-progress, *Meeting the Universe Halfway*); Astrid Schrader, "Temporal Ecologies and Political Phase-Spaces: Dinoflagellate Temporalities in Intra-action," paper for the October, 2005, meetings of the Society for Social Studies of Science.

5. Charis Thompson, *Making Parents: The Ontological Choreography of Reproductive Technologies* (Cambridge, MA: M.I.T. Press, 2005).

6. My own guess is that Dad fell because TB had already undermined his bones, not that TB was stimulated by falling. Interpretive options of this kind pepper telling any story, especially family stories. The line between fiction and fact runs through the living room.

7. I read about some of the secrets of the craft in a book I found in Dad's library after he died: Harry E. Heath, *How to Cover, Write, and Edit Sports* (Ames, Iowa: The Iowa State College Press, 1951). Sports covered: baseball, basketball, football, hockey, boxing, tennis. The baseball scoring system in this book seems much less nimble to me than Dad's. I would be surprised if Dad ever read Heath's tome.

V

Bodies and Violence

18

Hillbilly Armor and C-Legs: Technologies and Bodies at War[1]

Steve Kurzman

Introduction

If you are looking for a silver lining to the wars in Iraq and Afghanistan, allow me to suggest this: they will eventually lead to important advances in prosthetics technology and rehabilitative care for amputees. This ironic relationship is not a new development, although the ways in which it is currently being driven and embodied are new.

A specialized craft of making artificial limbs first emerged in the United States following the Civil War to cope with the amputees created by the war. This period also saw important technological innovations such as rubber feet. World War II also produced many American amputees and led to the birth of the modern, medicalized American prosthetics field through large-scale infrastructure development, as well as scientific and technical research. This "swords into plowshares" effect is different now, though: work on prosthetics and amputee rehabilitation has quietly been stepped up in the midst of the war. The Defense Department has not released data on how many amputations have resulted from the wars in Iraq and Afghanistan, but current estimates are that 6% of soldiers wounded in action have suffered amputations.[2] Nearly 15,000 soldiers had been wounded in action in Iraq as of the end of September 2005, so the numbers of amputations are still presumably very small: probably less than 1,000. For the sake of comparison, I would estimate, based on data from the Center for Disease Control, that over 200,000 Americans have had amputations resulting from complications of type II diabetes since the war in Iraq began.[3]

So, if sheer numbers are not driving the need for research and rehabilitation, as they did following previous wars, what is? I would suggest that it is the way in which this war is being fought. Iraq is the United States' first protracted engagement with urban guerilla warfare, and it is changing how bodies are wounded: American soldiers wounded in action in Iraq are at least twice as likely to survive their wounds than in previous wars, but are also twice as likely to become amputees and much more likely to suffer traumatic brain injuries. This paper briefly describes the interplay between Humvees, improvised explosive devices, and body armor in Iraq, and how it is wounding bodies in new ways.

Humvees

Politically speaking, the Iraq war began with two well-known blunders. One was the Pentagon's certainty that the initial combat phase of the invasion would be followed by an effort to win the hearts and minds of Iraqis. They failed to anticipate the insurgency. The second was that the Secretary of Defense was transforming the heavily armored military of the Cold War into a vision of a fast, light strike force. While this worked very well for the invasion of Iraq, it appears to have some drawbacks during the protracted urban guerilla warfare that has followed. American forces invaded Iraq in heavily armored tanks, but nothing says "occupation" like a tank, so soldiers were given Humvees in an effort to be more mobile and less obtrusive—and more able to engage with Iraqis.[4]

Humvees, or High-Mobility Multipurpose Wheeled Vehicles, were introduced in the mid-1980s and became the standard light tactical truck for the Army and Marines.[5] They are fast, rugged, and can be flexibly configured as troop carriers, weapons carriers, and even as ambulances.[6] But they are essentially very tough jeeps without substantial armor and were never intended to serve as armored personnel carriers in combat.[7] So when the insurgency began a few months after the invasion, one Marine officer pointed out the problem was that, "the war mutated from armored combat into a guerrilla campaign, and suddenly the tanks were parked and we moved out into the population without much protection."[8]

During the invasion, American soldiers encountered guns, mortars, and rocket-propelled grenades in combat, but insurgents started using improvised explosive devices, or IEDs, to attack vulnerable Humvees. IEDs are inexpensive to build, very effective against mounted soldiers (such as those in Humvees), and less risky than direct confrontation would be. As IED attacks on Humvees became more frequent, the Army quickly designed an add-on armor kit for them and increased production of a new, more heavily-armored model.[9] In the meantime, soldiers in Iraq began to build their own homemade armor, using scrap metal and ballistic glass cut to size.[10,11] This homemade version is commonly called "hillbilly" or "Mad Max" armor because of the junkyard aesthetic it introduces. Although up-armoring Humvees does add some protection, it also adds a thousand pounds to their weight and makes them slower, less mobile, and prone to break down more often due to the added stress.[12]

IEDs

Contrary to the Vice President's and Defense Secretary's assessments of the insurgents in Iraq as "dead enders" in their "last throes", they are sophisticated, organized, and adaptable. A recent article in the journal *Defense News*, based on interviews conducted at an Army conference on how to counter IEDs, describes small, non-hierarchical, independently operating IED cells that, in military parlance, are difficult to penetrate or decapitate. They have well-defined roles, and they both exchange skills and advertise their services over the internet. They conduct their own intelligence work by planting hoax IEDs and then studying how American soldiers respond to the perceived threats, and even videotape their attacks for study afterwards.[13]

American forces have been playing a game with these IED cells in which each seeks to adapt past the other. When Humvees were up-armored, IED cells countered by developing larger and more powerful bombs. Most IEDs early in the war were made from relatively small mortars. They now use much larger artillery shells and, in some cases, even aircraft bombs.[14] They also daisy-chain, or bundle, multiple artillery shells together, creating very powerful explosions capable of destroying armored Humvees and tanks.[15]

In the face of decreasing protection from armor, American forces organized a joint task force on IEDs to develop countermeasures.[16,17] One was to use electronic jamming devices to prevent IED triggermen from employing garage door openers and other radio control devices to detonate bombs. As insurgents broadened their range of devices to detonate bombs, such as cell phones, the Army purchased new electronic jammers that blocked the phones and a wider range of signals.[18,19] Early this summer, insurgents adapted again by starting to use infrared lasers as detonators or by returning to hardwiring the bombs.[20,21] Insurgents have also apparently received bomb-making assistance from colleagues in Hezbollah and the Iranian intelligence services, and are now starting to make armor-piercing shaped charges.[22] Another recent development is to mount IEDs off the ground, rather than underground, in order to increase their deadliness.[23]

IEDs are not only widely used—there are forty IED incidents on an average day in Iraq—but are an increasingly popular tactic of the insurgents.[24] There were no American fatalities due to IEDs during the first four months of the Iraq war. But during the remainder of 2003, 14% of American fatalities were caused by IEDs. The number increased to 22% in 2004, and then doubled to 45% in 2005. Last month, in September 2005, IEDs accounted for 75% of American fatalities and for many of the wounded. At this point, more American soldiers have been killed by IEDs than any other cause, including hostile fire.[25]

Body Armor

In addition to misjudging the appropriateness of Humvees, the Army also failed to anticipate the need for body armor. Initially, the Army outfitted only dismounted combat soldiers with body armor.[26] When the insurgency began using IEDs against supply convoys, it became clear that the line between dismounted combatants and mounted noncombatant soldiers was fuzzy, so Army vendors increased their production and eventually equipped all soldiers with body armor by January 2004—but not before many soldiers had purchased their own armor.[27]

The first body armor light enough to be used by American ground troops were flak jackets developed after World War II and used in the Korean War. A more heavily padded version of the same flak jacket was also used in the Vietnam War.[28] These flak jackets were made of ballistic nylon and, although fairly fragment resistant, were not actually bulletproof.[29] Body armor improved in the late 1970s and early 1980s, when police departments, and then the Army, started using a material called Kevlar, but the first two generations of Kevlar armor were too heavy.[30]

The current system, called Interceptor body armor, is both lighter weight at sixteen pounds, and more effective.[31] It is a vest made of Kevlar, with chest and back plate inserts made of a very hard ceramic material. The Interceptor body armor is truly bulletproof and its effectiveness borders on the bizarre at times. In one video made and originally posted to the web by Iraqi insurgents, an American medic is standing next to his Humvee. The crack of a sniper rifle is heard and the soldier drops to the ground, shot in the chest. He lays there for a couple seconds and then pops up, saved by his body armor, and takes cover behind his Humvee.[32] A recent article in Harper's relates a similar story:

"During a battle along the mountain ridges of Tora Bora, Afghanistan, in 2002, a Special Forces trooper was shot at close range by a Taliban fighter: three rounds from an AK-47 to the GI's chest. The soldier dropped to the ground, and a few moments later stood up again to shoot and kill his attacker. According to those who were there, it was like seeing Lazarus rise from the dead."[33]

However, while body armor protects the soldier's chest and abdomen—their core mass—it does nothing to protect their heads, faces, or limbs. Army researchers are working on designs to add upper arm, shoulder, and leg modules to the Interceptor body armor and to develop liquid body armor which could be used in uniforms to protect limbs.[34,35] But in the meantime, we are now fighting a war in which soldiers can survive being shot at close range with an AK-47, but are increasingly having their limbs blown off of their unscathed torsos by IEDs. The tragic interplay of IEDs, body armor, and battlefield medicine is radically changing how soldiers are killed and their bodies are wounded.

Wounded Bodies

Like body armor, battlefield medicine has much improved since the Vietnam War, in terms of speed as well as treatment.[36] Forward Surgical Teams, the modern version of MASH units, travel in Humvees and treat wounded soldiers very close to the battlefield. The wounded are then moved to Combat Support Hospitals and subsequently to hospitals in Kuwait, Spain, and Germany if needed. Seriously wounded troops are quickly flown back to the United States—on average, within four days of being wounded.[37] The survival rate compares favorably with previous wars: 90% of soldiers wounded in action survive their wounds, compared with only 76% in the Vietnam War or 70% in WW2.[38]

However, the wounds are terrible. Army surgeons report relatively few chest and abdomen wounds due to the body armor, but many head, face, and neck wounds, as well as "an unprecedented burden of what orthopedists term "mangled extremities".[39] Although soldiers wounded in action in Iraq are more likely to survive, the number of amputations is, by recent estimates, twice that of previous wars.[40] In addition, 20% of the amputees have lost more than one limb and 35% have lost an arm[41] (compared to approximately 10% of civilian amputees).

Less visible, but very common, is the traumatic brain injuries, or TBI. Doctors at Walter Reed Army Medical Center have begun screening all soldiers wounded in explosions, vehicle accidents, falls, or by gunshot wounds to the face, neck, and head, and have found TBI in roughly 60% of the cases[42] (compared to 12-14% in Vietnam).[43] Although the Kevlar helmets protect against penetrating wounds from fragments and bullets, they cannot protect soldiers' brains from the concussive injuries resulting from massive IED explosions.[44]

Prostheses

The Defense Department has apparently noticed the effects of this war on bodies and is responding by building amputee care centers, funding prosthetics research, and supplying amputee veterans with state-of-the-art prostheses. In January 2005, the Army opened a second amputee care center at Brooke Army Medical Center in San Antonio (the first is at Walter Reed Army Medical Center in Washington) and will probably open a third center in San Diego in the future.[45, 46]

The army had also planned to build a Military Amputee Training Center at Walter Reed, but construction stopped after Walter Reed was slated for closure. The Center was to have a unique mission: to be at least partially devoted to retraining soldiers with amputations to return to combat. Just as well-designed rehabilitation centers in civilian hospitals often include mockups of kitchens, laundry rooms, supermarkets, and other scenes of daily life, the Military Amputee Training Center was to include obstacle courses, tank and terrain simulations, and weapons training for amputees.[47] This seems to signal that the Defense Department is conceptualizing wounded bodies differently and sees them as much more recuperable than previously. Instead, another rehabilitation center will be built in San Antonio—without the military training capability—but soldiers are returning to active duty after disabling wounds nevertheless.[48]

The Defense Department has also begun to fund prosthetics research. The projects are all rather futuristic and not likely to yield usable results in the near future, though they will probably be important in stimulating future development. The focus appears to be on upper-extremity prostheses, presumably because of the high proportion of soldiers losing arms and because the quality of artificial arms lags behind that of legs. The Defense Advanced Research Projects Agency, or DARPA, is working to develop "a complete prosthetic upper extremity with full motor and sensory function" that will "function as well as a normal human arm" and be operated by neural control.[49] This is ambitious, to say the least, and they have also proposed a shorter-term project to simply improve upon currently available arms.[50] Brown University and MIT are also partnering to create a bio-hybrid prosthesis using tissue generation, bone lengthening, osseo-integration of titanium fixtures, and implanted sensors that assist neural control of prostheses—also rather ambitious.[51,52]

In the meantime, until the troops can be bio-hybridized, the Defense Department is equipping amputees with high quality prostheses. The C-Leg for above-knee amputees, in particular, has received much attention in the press and in the Doonesbury cartoon series, where the character B.D. received one after losing one of his legs above the knee. The C-Leg is interesting because it is the first "context-aware" prosthesis in the sense that it is aware of how it is being used and adjusts accordingly. A difficulty in using above-knee prostheses is how to maintain stability during stance and swing phases of the gait cycle, or when one's heel hits the ground and when the leg swings forward for the next step. The C-Leg has sensors that collect data on the user's gait and a micro-processor that helps control the stance and swing phases of gait, making walking a more natural and less conscious process.[53] Otto Bock, a German prosthetics company founded after World War I, introduced the C-Leg in 1999, but it has received much wider distribution (and an enormous amount of publicity) since the war in Iraq began.

What does all of this mean, especially here at home in the United States? The research initiatives are ambitious, but will probably lead to significant advances in prosthetics in the distant future, which may benefit the large numbers of Baby Boomers likely to lose limbs to diabetes. For now, the C-Leg promises to lead the prosthetics field into context-aware technology. And the tragic relationship between IEDs and defensive technologies such as Humvees and body armor provoke disturbing questions about how soldiers are dying and bodies are wounded in even more horrifically violent ways.

Economically, though, we will also feel the impact of this technological interplay in the high cost of rehabilitation for wounded soldiers. C-Legs are not cheap—they cost over $30,000—and like any prosthetic limb, they must be replaced every few years over the lifetime of the amputee. The Department of Defense pays for the rehabilitation of soldiers while they are on active duty, but that burden shifts to employer-sponsored healthcare or the Department of Veterans Affairs when disabled soldiers are discharged. Veterans Affairs not only has a history of being chronically underfunded, but is currently plagued by budgetary ineptness: they seriously underestimated the numbers of veterans from the wars in Iraq and Afghanistan who require medical and rehabilitation treatment and the Senate had to pass an emergency appropriation of $1.5 billion to cover a huge shortfall.[54,55,56] Not only has current care suffered, but the VA has seen its budget for prosthetics research gradually reduced during the current war.[57,58]

Much of the public attention to the wars in Afghanistan and Iraq has been focused on the dazzling or inadequate qualities of technology in combat, be it the "shock and awe" of precision bombing or dangerously vulnerable Humvees. Let us also turn our attention to the long-term consequences and costs of these technologies—and perhaps more importantly, to their impacts upon the bodies of our fellow soldier citizens.

Notes

1. I would like to thank Prof. Nancy N. Chen for inviting me to present at the *Body Modifications* conference and for including my essay in this volume. Of course, I am solely responsible for the contents of this essay, and can be contacted at info@ethnographic-consulting.com. All arguments and conclusions presented in this essay are based on current events in October 2005.

2. There are actually two different rates of amputation being cited in the mainstream media and, curiously, both are described as being twice the rate of amputations suffered in previous wars. Many media accounts cite the 6% figure, for example:

"Data compiled by the US Senate, and included in the 2005 defense appropriations bill in support of a request for increased funding for the care of amputees at Walter Reed Army Medical Center, reveal that 6 percent of those wounded in Iraq have required amputations, compared with a rate of 3 percent for past wars." (Mishra Raja, "Amputation rate for US troops twice that of past wars: Doctors cite need for prosthetics as more lives saved.," *The Boston Globe*, December 9 2004, available at www. boston.com/news/world/articles/2004/12/09/amputation_rate_for_us _troops_twice_that_of_past_wars/, accessed on September 30, 2005.)

As of mid-2004, Charles Scoville, Program Manager for the U.S. Army Amputee Patient Care Program, reported to the House Committee on Veterans Affairs that "during the current conflict, amputations account for 2.4% of all WIA." (House Committee on Veterans Affairs, *Statement by Mr. Chuck Scoville, Hearing on the Evolution of VA-DoD Collaboration in Research and Amputee Care for Veterans of Current and Past Conflicts, as well as Needed Reforms in VA Blind Rehabilitation Services*, July 22 2004, available at veterans.house.gov/hearings/schedule108/jul04/7-22-04/cscoville.html, accessed on September 30, 2005.)

3. According to the Center for Disease Control, the annual number of "Hospital Discharges for Nontraumatic Lower Extremity Amputation with Diabetes as a Listed Diagnosis" has remained over 80,000 since 1997 (National Diabetes Surveillance System National Center for Chronic Disease Prevention and Health Promotion, "Hospitalizations for Nontraumatic Lower Extremity Amputation," (2005), available at www.cdc.gov/diabetes/statistics/lea/fig1.htm, accessed on September 30, 2005.). Accordingly, I used a conservative estimate of 80,000

amputees per year since Operation Iraqi Freedom began in March 2003 to arrive at the figure of at least 200,000 amputees due to diabetes in that time period.

4. Jeffrey Sorenson Major General Stephen Speakes, Colonel John Rooney, "Special Defense Department Briefing on Uparmoring HMMWV," (U.S. Dept of Defense, Office of the Assistant Secretary of Defense (Public Affairs), 2004), available at www.dod.mil/transcripts/2004/tr20041215 -1801.html, accessed on September 30, 2005.

5. Sandra I. Erwin, "Tactical Trucks for Tomorrow's Army: Can Commercial Vehicles Do the Job?," *National Defense* 2001, available at www.nationaldefensemagazine.org/issues/2001/Apr/Tactical_Trucks .htm, accessed on September 30, 2005.

6. Army Public Affairs, "HMMWV," in *Army Fact File*, available at www .army.mil/fact_files_site/hmmwv/, accessed on September 30, 2005.

7. John Barry, Babak Dehghanpisheh and Michael Hirsh, "'Hillbilly Armor': Defense sees it's fallen short in securing the troops. The grunts already knew.," *Newsweek*, December 20 2004, available at www.msnbc .msn.com/id/6700920/site/newsweek/, accessed on September 30, 2005.

8. Michael Moran, "Frantically, the Army tries to armor Humvees: Soft-skinned workhorses turning into death traps," *MSNBC*, April 15, 2004, available at www.msnbc.msn.com/id/4731185/, accessed on September 30, 2005.

9. John Barry and Babak Dehghanpisheh Michael Hirsh, "'Hillbilly Armor': Defense sees it's fallen short in securing the troops. The grunts already knew," *Newsweek*, December 20, 2004, available at www.msnbc .msn.com/id/6700920/site/newsweek/, accessed on September 30, 2005.

10. "Troops Scavenge Scrap Metal to Protect Combat Vehicles," (ABC News, 2004), available at abcnews.go.com/WNT/story?id=312959&page=1, accessed on September 30, 2005.

11. John Barry and Babak Dehghanpisheh Michael Hirsh, "'Hillbilly Armor': Defense sees it's fallen short in securing the troops. The grunts already knew," *Newsweek*, December 20, 2004, available at www.msnbc .msn.com/id/6700920/site/newsweek/, accessed on September 30, 2005.

12. Jeffrey Sorenson Major General Stephen Speakes, Colonel John Rooney, "Special Defense Department Briefing on Uparmoring HMMWV," (U.S. Dept of Defense, Office of the Assistant Secretary of Defense (Public Affairs), 2004), available at www.dod.mil/transcripts/ 2004/tr20041215-1801.html, accessed on September 30, 2005.

John Barry and Babak Dehghanpisheh Michael Hirsh, "'Hillbilly Armor': Defense sees it's fallen short in securing the troops. The grunts already knew.," *Newsweek*, December 20 2004, available at www.msnbc .msn.com/id/6700920/site/newsweek/, accessed on September 30, 2005.

13. Greg Grant, "Inside Iraqi Insurgent Cells, Captured Terrorist Intel May Help Defeat IED," *Defense News* (2005), available at staging .defensenews.com/story.php?F=999446&C=mideast, accessed on September 30, 2005.

14. Greg Grant, "Death Toll Sparks U.S. Debate On Origin of IED Expertise in Iraq," *Defense News*, August 15, 2005, available at staging.defensenews .com/story.php?F=949750&C=america, accessed on September 30, 2005.

15. Mark Washburn, "More Americans Dying from Roadside Bombs in Iraq," (Knight-Ridder, 2005), available at www.commondreams.org/ headlines05/0610-05.htm, accessed on September 30, 2005.

16. Rey Guzman, "Joint IED Task Force helping defuse insurgency's threat," (ARNews Army News Service, 2005), available at www.global security.org/military/library/news/2005/07/mil-050718-arnews02.htm, accessed on September 30, 2005.

17. Sgt. 1st Class Doug Sample, "IED Conference Looks for Solutions to Save Lives," (American Forces Information Service, 2005), available at www.defenselink.mil/news/May2005/20050504_889.html, accessed on September 30, 2005.

18. Mark Washburn, "More Americans Dying from Roadside Bombs in Iraq," (Knight-Ridder, 2005), available at www.commondreams.org/ headlines05/0610-05.htm, accessed on September 30, 2005.

19. Greg Grant, "Inside Iraqi Insurgent Cells, Captured Terrorist Intel May Help Defeat IED," *Defense News* (2005), available at staging.defensenews .com/story.php?F=999446&C=mideast, accessed on September 30, 2005.

20. David S. Cloud, "Iraqi Rebels Refine Bomb Skills, Pushing Toll of GI's Higher," *The New York Times*, June 22 2005, available at www .occupationwatch.org/headlines/archives/2005/06/iraqi_rebels_re.html, accessed on September 30, 2005.

21. Melissa Block, "Iraq's Insurgents Turn to Infrared Triggers," (NPR, 2005), available at www.npr.org/templates/story/story.php?storyId=4714571, accessed on September 30, 2005.

22. Greg Grant, "Inside Iraqi Insurgent Cells, Captured Terrorist Intel May Help Defeat IED," *Defense News* (2005), available at staging.defense news.com/story.php?F=999446&C=mideast, accessed on September 30, 2005.

23. James Dunnigan, "The IED War in Iraq," (Strategy Page, 2005), available at www.strategypage.com/dls/articles/200541410.asp, accessed on September 30, 2005.

24. Greg Grant, "Inside Iraqi Insurgent Cells, Captured Terrorist Intel May Help Defeat IED," *Defense News* (2005), available at staging.defensenews .com/story.php?F=999446&C=mideast, accessed on September 30, 2005.

25. All statistics of American casualties in this paragraph were based on data from the online database "Iraqi Coalition Casualty Count," available at icasualties.org/oif/, accessed on October 13, 2005.

26. Vernon Loeb and Theola Labbé, "Body armor saves U.S. lives in Iraq: Pentagon criticized for shortage of protective vests," *The Washington Post*, December 4, 2003, available at www.msnbc.com/news/1000971 .asp?cp1=1, accessed on September 30, 2005.

27. Michael Moss, "Many Missteps Tied to Delay Of Armor to Protect Soldiers," *The New York Times*, March 7 2005, available at www.globalsecurity.org/org/news/2005/050307-armor-missteps.htm, accessed on September 30, 2005.

28. Olive-Drab, "U.S. Military Body Armor: Vietnam Flak Vest," available at www.olive-drab.com/od_soldiers_gear_body_armor_vietnam.php, accessed on September 30, 2005.

29. Olive-Drab, "U.S. Military Body Armor (Flak Jackets)," available at www.olive-drab.com/od_soldiers_gear_body_armor_korea.php, accessed on September 30, 2005.

30. Mary Bellis, "History of Body Armor and Bullet Proof Vests," (About.com), available at inventors.about.com/od/bstartinventions/a/ Body_Armor.htm, accessed on September 30, 2005.

31. Seth Stern, "Body armor could be a technological hero of war in Iraq," *The Christian Science Monitor*, April 2, 2003, available at www. csmonitor.com/2003/0402/p04s01-usmi.html, accessed on September 30, 2005.

32. "U.S. Soldier Survives Sniper Attack," (2005), available at www.ogrish .com/archives/us_soldier_survives_sniper_attack_Jul_16_2005.html, accessed on September 30, 2005.

33. Ronald J. Glasser, "A war of disabilities: Iraq's hidden costs are coming home," *Harper's Magazine*, August 12, 2005, available at uslaboragainstwar .org/article.php?id=8862&printsafe=1, accessed on September 30, 2005.

34. "Ballistic Protection to Counter the Effects of the Improvised Explosive Devices (IED) Threat," available at nsc.natick.army.mil/media/ fact/individual/IED_Protection.htm, accessed on September 30, 2005.

35. Tonya Johnson, "Army scientists, engineers develop liquid body armor," *Army News Service*, April 21, 2004, available at www4.army.mil/ ocpa/read.php?story_id_key=5872, accessed on September 30, 2005.

36. Dan Ferber, "Soldiers of Fortune?: Innovations in battlefield medicine are ensuring that more combatants survive. Often, the technology follows them home," *Popular Science* 2005, available at www.popsci.com/ popsci/science/49a20b4511b84010vgnvcm1000004eecbccdrcrd.html, accessed on September 30, 2005.

37. M. D. Atul Gawande, M.P.H., "Casualties of War — Military Care for the Wounded from Iraq and Afghanistan," *The New England Journal of Medicine* 351, no. 24, available at content.nejm.org/cgi/content/full/351/24/2471, accessed on September 30, 2005.

38. *Ibid.*

39. *Ibid.*

40. Mishra Raja, "Amputation rate for US troops twice that of past wars: Doctors cite need for prosthetics as more lives saved.," *The Boston Globe*, December 9, 2004, available at www.boston.com/news/world/articles/2004/12/09/amputation_rate_for_us_troops_twice_that_of_past_wars/, accessed on September 30, 2005.

41. "Executive Summary, Prosthetic Fitting & Adjustment Clinical Working Group, Traumatic Amputation QUERI Workshop," (Department of Veterans Affairs, 2004), available at www.vard.org/meet/queri/groups/fitting.pdf, accessed on September 30, 2005.

42. Gregg Zoroya, "Key Iraq wound: Brain trauma," *USA Today*, March 3, 2005, available at www.usatoday.com/news/nation/2005-03-03-brain-trauma-lede_x.htm, accessed on September 30, 2005.

43. Susan Okie M.D., "Traumatic Brain Injury in the War Zone," *The New England Journal of Medicine* 352, no. 20 (2005), available at content.nejm.org/cgi/content/full/352/20/2043, accessed on September 30, 2005.

44. Matthew B. Stannard, "The invisible wound: Though high-tech body armor saves lives on the battlefield, more and more troops are suffering traumatic head injuries," *San Francisco Chronicle*, July 14, 2004, available at www.sfgate.com/cgi-bin/article.cgi?file=/chronicle/archive/2004/07/14/MNGGE7L6971.DTL, accessed on September 30, 2005.

45. Staff Sgt. Reeba Critser, "Texas opens Army's second Amputee Center," (ARNews Army News Service, 2005), available at www4.army.mil/ocpa/read.php?story_id_key=6756, accessed on September 30, 2005.

46. "More injured troops are surviving," *Colorado Springs Gazette*, February 13, 2005, available at www.gazette.com/war/0213warxxa.html, accessed on September 30, 2005.

47. Bernard S. Little, "Walter Reed breaks ground for amputee training center," (ARNews Army News Service, 2004), available at www4.army.mil/ocpa/read.php?story_id_key=6582, accessed on September 30, 2005.

48. Sarah Baxter, "Bionic US troops go back to war," *The Sunday Times*, March 13 2005, available at www.timesonline.co.uk/article/0,,2089-1522894,00.html, accessed on September 30, 2005.

49. DARPA/DSO, "Revolutionizing Prosthetics Presolicitation Notice," (2005), available at www.darpa.mil/baa/baa05-26.html, accessed on September 30, 2005.

50. DARPA/DSO, "Prosthesis 2007 Presolicitation Notice," (2005), available at www.darpa.mil/baa/baa05-19mod5.htm, accessed on September 30, 2005.

51. Brown University, The News Service, "VA Funds Leading-Edge Limb-Loss Research in Providence" (2004), available at www.brown.edu/Administration/News_Bureau/2004-05/04-061.html, accessed on September 30, 2005.

52. "VA Funds New Limb-Loss Research" (U.S. Department of Veterans Affairs, 2004), available at www1.va.gov/opa/pressrel/PressArtInternet.cfm?id=925, accessed on September 30, 2005.

53. "C-Leg: New Generation Leg System Revolutionizes Lower Limb Prostheses" (Otto Bock HealthCare), available at www.ottobockus.com/products/lower_limb_prosthetics/c-leg_article.asp, accessed on September 30, 2005.

54. Thomas B. Edsall, "Funds for Health Care of Veterans $1 Billion Short: 2005 Deficit Angers Senate Republicans, Advocacy Groups," *The Washington Post*, June 24, 2005, available at www.washingtonpost.com/wp-dyn/content/article/2005/06/23/AR2005062301888.html, accessed on September 30, 2005.

55. Thomas B. Edsall, "VA Faces $2.6 Billion Shortfall in Medical Care: Agency Undercounted Size of Returning Force," *The Washington Post*, June 29, 2005, available at www.washingtonpost.com/wp-dyn/content/article/2005/06/28/AR2005062800545.html, accessed on September 30, 2005.

56. Associated Press, "Senate Approves Additional Money for Veterans' Health Care," *The Washington Post*, June 30, 2005, available at www.washingtonpost.com/wp-dyn/content/article/2005/07/29/AR2005072901816.html, accessed on September 30, 2005.

57. "FY 2005 Budget Proposal Falls Short For Research" (The American Physiological Society Legislative Action Center), available at www.the-aps.org/pa/action/fy2005/FY05Budget.htm, accessed on September 30, 2005.

58. "Bush Budget? Bummer!" (The American Psychological Association), available at www.apa.org/ppo/issues/fy06budget.html, accessed on September 30, 2005.

19

Nursing Memory:
Who Deserves to Heal
and After Which War(s)?[1]

Megan Moodie

Stories of return from war are often narratives of citizenship. They retain a great deal of moral weight as cultural forms, a weight in part derived from the implied risk to the body in the name of dedication to country, and they compel collective listening in ways that the stories of those others of war—civilian victims, the "enemy"—simply do not. Because they seem to be told in a unified voice, differences, as they emerge, are striking. As such, veterans' stories tell us a great deal about how bodies are positioned in relation to the categories that make a difference within the nation-state: race, class, gender.

Until the first Gulf War, women who were in the military most often served as nurses. In World War II, 59,000 American women served as nurses in the Army and Navy Corps. At least 10,000 served in various capacities in Vietnam, most of them as nurses. These veterans have return tales that deserve a great deal more attention than they have received for the ways in which they not only tell us about women's experiences in and with the military, but also for what these narratives say about our definitions of citizenship, of gendered citizenship. Nurses' stories of return from war tell us about who deserves care—

nursing, attention to welfare and well-being—and under what conditions. We see quickly that not everyone in the nation-state is deserving in the same way, that not every wound can be nursed. What kind of suffering makes a citizen?

More importantly, which stories of suffering entitle individuals to citizen benefits? I propose that inducements for women veterans to tell the truth about the risks of military service for women, especially beginning in Vietnam—to tell stories of trauma—have been reappropriated by the military itself to such an extent that there is very little space for women in the military to speak against the kind of gender-encoding that marks them as always less-than-male soldiers and at special risk for trauma by virtue of their inherent vulnerability In other words, as women veterans have begun to tell stories about assault, abuse, and harassment within the armed forces—a kind of truth-telling to be lauded by most feminists—their institutional truth-telling has been taken over and militarized. Further, while their narratives seem to be painfully individuated, they are also about welfare, about what kind of care *women* veterans, as opposed to a generic, non-embodied veteran, might need. Consider the following stories. "It was different then," Sharon Connelly tells me over lunch at the Monterey Seniors' Center. Sharon is a veteran, a Junior Grade Lieutenant in the Navy who served as a nurse for two years in World War II, including six months at Pearl Harbor in 1945. "You saw a need and you filled it. People now are trained to be administrators, not nurses. In World War II, everyone knew they were in it together." As we chew our Meals on Wheels Swedish meatballs, Sharon recounts one story that she remembers very clearly, told to her by a young Navy Medical Corpsman. They were in Pearl Harbor. The Corpsman met an incoming ship and another young sailor stumbled off screaming "I'm dying! I'm dying! Please give me medicine for the pain!" The Corpsman gave the sailor a shot of morphine and shortly thereafter the sailor slumped over and died. When Sharon met the Corpsman, later being treated on her psychiatric ward for combat fatigue, he couldn't get over the idea that he had killed this man. Sharon tried to comfort the Corpsman by telling him that he had been following his training and had done the right thing, that the man's death was not his fault. She also informed the psychiatrist who was treating the Corpsman about his extreme feelings of guilt. "The doctors counted on us doing little things like this," she says. The "fellas," as she calls them, confided in their nurses. "You saw a need and you filled it. Wife, sweetheart, mother, sister. A good war nurse is all these things. She has to be." Sharon remembers her service in World War II as the happiest time of her life. The nurses respected the soldiers, who needed them. Everyone was in this together and even if there are awful stories to tell of the pain of the sailor and the Corpsman, the larger story of return is one of meaning, purpose, even enjoyment.

Compare Sharon's story with that of Lily, an Army Nurse veteran who served in Vietnam, captured in the film *No Time for Tears*[2]:

> When I got there, half the ward were men that had usually double amputations with complications. . . . When you work twelve hours a day, six days a week with these men you start to become friends with them. They're not just patients. They become your social network. I'd hear about their babies and their young wives at home and then they would die on me. And I found that just so painful.

Her fellow-nurse Kathy recounts the following reaction upon the death of a staff nurse in an air strike:

> I hadn't internalized it that I wanted it to be me. I couldn't say that at the time—that I didn't want to be there anymore. That I didn't want to be hurt anymore. I didn't want any more lies to be told to me. 'Cause Susan died and I was told that nurses didn't die. And she died in a bombing.

Or consider the statement of Joann, a veteran who was treated at the country's only inpatient center for women veterans suffering from Post-Traumatic Stress Disorder often as the result of what is known in the Veterans' Administration as

Military Sexual Trauma, or MST, and whose story appears on the center's Web site:

> I felt broken and damaged. . . . I wanted my life back—the way it was before the night I was incomprehensibly raped, robbed and then raped again. . . .The thought of having to live the rest of my life with PTSD was incredibly haunting.

Surely, despite their close relationship with the male soldiers, service does not represent the best time in Lily, Kathy, or Joann's lives. War is something from which they have to recover.

The coexistence of such different narratives within the discursive terrain of the "woman veteran," one of heterosexual romance and the other of trauma and tentative recovery, challenges us to think about historical shifts in American cultural notions about the suffering caused by war that tells us a great deal about gendered citizenship. If nurses in World War II had to heal the mentally fatigued and physically injured, in Lily, Kathy and Joann's cases, the healers became those in need of healing. It would be easy to tell stories of progress about these cases in which concerted effort by women in the name of "women in the military" brought about greater awareness of the emotional stresses of combat and the prevalence of sexual violence in the military. *These things used to happen, but were repressed. People just didn't talk about them. Now the military is forced to deal with the reality of women's difficulties in a masculine institution.* We might also attempt a story of decline in which an earlier notion or set of practices called "chivalry" kept women away from harm by their enemies or comrades. *These things just did not happen, and the death of chivalry has put women at greater risk.* The first progress narrative problematically implies that things have always been like they are; the second decline narrative tries to fool us into thinking that there was an era of "gentlemanly" war and violence. I propose that we think about Sharon's "best job ever" and Lily, Kathy, and Joann's return narratives not in terms of truth-telling about the past. Some therapists and concerned commentators would probably be inclined to question whether Sharon had not repressed other, perhaps painful, aspects of her time in the Navy. Many feminists would remind us, however, that we must balance the incitement to speech about rape and horror with respect for silence; the question of "fact" itself reproduces the idea that somehow revealing the truth can make deeply cultured forms of violence go away. We know that nurses were in combat situations even when these were not recognized as combat, that they were tortured as prisoners of war, and both civilian and military women were sexually assaulted. Truth-telling does not seem to have changed military—or civilian—practices a great deal.

There is an important historical relationship between the two nursing narratives, however, despite their obvious differences, which points towards a set of concerns that go to the heart of what citizen rights can be expected by women in the United States. In the nurses' stories we hear the elaboration of cultural notions of welfare, of whose bodies and minds deserve nursing and support and under what conditions. During Sharon's service in the Navy, the United States was in the midst of reconstructing its welfare state. While the New Deal of the 1930s reinforced a conventional division of labor—the male breadwinner and female homemaker—that excluded racial minorities and defined motherhood as central to women's citizenship, it attempted to create social services for the general population. At least in theory, the Depression affected everyone and everyone needed assistance. Citizenship itself meant access to social services: we're all in this together.

Late in World War II, a decisive break was made by a coalition of Republicans and Southern Democrats to roll back the social programs of the New Deal. The result was the GI Bill, passed in 1944, as a promise to *soldiers* that their service had been important and that they and their families would be taken care of. This had the effect of creating a differential citizenship under that assigned welfare rights only to those who served in the military, and wedded the idea of collective well-being, welfare, to the military imperative of national security.[3] Sharon benefited from the GI Bill; to go to college, she merely had to show her service documents. Surely in her assertion that everyone got taken care of, we also hear her "success" through military service and her sense of belonging to a generation.

Since the inauguration of the post-Vietnam All-Volunteer Force, the rift between civilian and military life has been growing.[4] Real citizenship is still in many ways contingent on military service and a particular kind of suffering for the nation-state, especially in electoral politics. Those who do not serve in the military (it is only 15% women at the most) are always less-than-ideal citizens. Yet, at the same moment when women and minorities are gaining "equality" in the military, it is also losing cultural capital so that gender and race privilege can be maintained. Women *veterans*, I would argue, occupy a difficult space between these two worlds. Even while they have access to resources that civilian women do not have by virtue of their special citizenship, there are very specific narrative frames through which they must tell their stories to retain that citizenship; specifically, that of trauma of the kind narrated by Lily, Kathy, and Joann. "Trauma" personalizes the suffering of war and takes the "military" out of Military Sexual Trauma even as it seems to "open up" women's experiences of war.[5]

We cannot leave aside the important question of race in any analysis either of women veterans' narratives or questions of differential citizenship. African-American women are disproportionately represented both in the military and in the cultural imagination of welfare. It is telling that African-American women even *in* the military have a harder time claiming benefits than their white peers. Shoshana Johnson, the African-American cook who was captured along with blond icon Jessica Lynch in Iraq was given 30% disability while Jessica was given 80%, despite the fact that the result of Shoshana's injuries—bullets in both ankles—was more permanent. The irony stands as a painful symbol of exactly the kind of constellation I am trying to unravel here.

Military women can "prove" that a wound has been inflicted in the name of the nation-state, whether it is Sharon happily nursing the wounds of the fellas or Lily, Kathy, and Joann suffering from PTSD after their own nursing tours. We have no such processes for the poor to prove their wounds in the same name. There are no nurses for victims from other kinds of wars. We have no language to articulate the ways in which the sexual trauma of all women—regardless of whether they get intensive inpatient care in a VA facility—or feminized poverty also serve the interests of a violence and masculinized state that depends on male aggression and female dependence. Such speech becomes impossible in a discursive universe that relies on notions of undifferentiated citizenship; suffering is always pathological, not systemic, and individually, not socially, encoded.

"Trauma" seems off the mark, as I have tried to show in this brief essay, with its heavy reliance on the notion of the individual at the expense of recognizing social conditions that traumatize and in its implicit incitement to speech. What we have gained in terms of "truth" about the sexualized violence of war since World War II we have lost in terms of the recognition that, to paraphrase Gwendolyn Mink, welfare is a condition of equality.[6] Only a certain kind of suffering makes a citizen entitled to well-being, and women—veteran women, poor women, women of color, all women—have only fleeting access to it, and only if they agree to locate the trauma inside themselves, rather than in society at large. Turning their experiences into trauma narratives in effect gives with one hand while taking away with the other; women may be acknowledged to be traumatized in war (not only because of what war is, but because of the prevalence of sexual violence in war), but this is a personal problem. As such, though it may be singularly devastating, it has no relationship to the more generalized forms of suffering wrought by a militarized world. We need only to think of the recent horror in New Orleans to remind ourselves that in terms of recognizing the humanity of all of its citizens, the US has failed, and continues to fail, in grave ways. The fallout of Hurricane Katrina should alert us strongly to the ways in which social disasters are made "natural," sentimental (and therefore individual), and apolitical. We need, I think, to regroup.

Notes

1. I am grateful to Nancy Chen, John Marlovits, Helene Moglen, Anna Tsing, and Bahiyyih Watson for advice and comments on earlier drafts of this essay.

2. *No Time for Tears: Vietnam, the women who served*. Directed by Elizabeth Bouiss. West End Films. Distributed by The Video Project, Ben Lomond, California, 1993.

3. Sherry, Michael. *In the Shadow of War: The United States Since the 1930s*. New Haven and London: Yale University Press, 1982.

4. See Lutz, Katherine. *Homefront: A Military City and the American Twentieth Century*. Boston: Beacon Press, 2001. It is important to keep in mind that this separation is only at the scale of an imagined national body. In contemporary US culture, some communities are located as mines from which soldierly bodies will be drawn. Here, there is no separation at all between military and civilian life. We might think of Fayetteville, North Carolina, American Samoa, or certain neighborhoods of San Diego, California. Many thanks to Nicole Santos for helping to clarify my thinking on this issue.

5. In fact, I was told by the head of a VA mental health center for women that the military part of the diagnosis matters very little; instead, it is an administrative category that determines benefit entitlements.

6. Mink, Gwendolyn. *Welfare's End*. Ithaca and London: Cornell University Press, 1998.

20

Dead Bodies, Violence, and Living On through Plastination

Nancy N. Chen

Medicine offers a powerful lens onto the human condition. The medical gaze, in particular, has become a common entry point into the human body. Early anatomical sketches by da Vinci, schematic maps of Chinese acupuncture points, and Victorian paintings of dissected bodies offer medicalized visions that eventually come to represent human bodies to larger lay audiences. Contemporary US television and news media offer an array of medical and forensic dramas with the hospital ward, dissection room, or plastic surgery operating table as primary sites for the viewing of bodies. Vivid images of laboratory dissections or operating techniques are interspersed with ongoing story plots. These ways of seeing, via dead bodies and their parts, offer the perfect body—one that can be dissected, mapped, and reframed. In the past three decades, the literature on bodies addresses lived experience and subjective knowledge through embodiment or rejection of that somatic frame. Few, with the exception of Cartwright (1997) in her analysis of the visible human project, address the impact of dead bodies and how these come to represent the living. This paper examines the stories that are told about dead bodies through new technologies of viewing. In the horror genre, a dead body in daily life often represents evil or an immoral order. However, science and medicine have come to offer a different representation: one that is quite human and accepted as an embodiment of the universal being.

Plastination is a recent technique that enables corpses to be preserved without formaldehyde, which tended to transform the color of tissue and organs in toxic fumes. With plastination, the fat and water in human tissue and various body parts are removed and the body is then slowly injected with polymers. This form of preservation, which slows down decomposition, was patented in the 1970s by Dr. Gunther von Hagens, an eccentric Austrian scientist who then went on to create large scale exhibits of plastinated bodies. These exhibitions—*Körperweltern* or BodyWorlds, Inc.—have traveled across Europe, Asia, and now North America since the 1990s. Von Hagens's process is rarely coded as violent. Instead, it is framed in the medical culture as preservative and in the popular media as a fascinating opportunity to look inside.

In what follows, I attempt to trace the flow of plastinated bodies upstream from the popular exhibition halls, their production in plastination factories and, ultimately, to the donor bodies that enable this circulation. In the process, I address the management of dead bodies and query their different paths from the organ trade. Cadaveric bodies donated to science in order to further medical education live on as social objects of public display in new ways. The procurement and use of cadavers raises questions about what happens to dead bodies that are not necessarily organized by donation. As in Victorian times, there is a concern that lurks behind such exhibits: have cadaveric bodies originated from questionable sources such as prisons and morgues? Beyond these immediate issues of the ethics of donation or the presumed violence of cadaveric origins, I am also curious about what it is that we see when such bodies are on display and what stories they tell about our culture of medicine. In some displays, disfigurement, dismemberment, and disembowelment are presented as natural forms of representation, while in other exhibits elaborate efforts are made to contextualize the plastinated cadaver in daily life or in practices that disrupt the distancing that takes place between life and afterlife.

"I see dead bodies"

My first encounter with plastinated cadaveric bodies was in 2001. Dramatic posters of a dissected male body sitting on a dissected horse could be seen all over Berlin. Given the history of medical experimentation during the Nazi regime, it was disconcerting to see these posters advertising "Anatomy Art." Would this be a Barnum and Bailey show of oddities? Repulsed yet curious, I decided to visit the exhibit on a Wednesday evening with Afsaneh Kalantary, a University of California Santa Cruz graduate student then finishing field work in Berlin. Housed in a former railway station of East Berlin, the exhibit had about 200 preserved bodies, with one horse and eight fetuses. Only two of the figures were female and both were pregnant with the plastinated fetus also visible. Many of the bodies had tattoos still evident on their arms and even more had blackened lungs.

The display of bodies was fascinating to view. Some were posed in various activities, engaged in a sport, for example, or hunched over a keyboard. Having suffered a recent knee injury, I was amazed to see an anterior cruciate ligament (ACL) on one body. More fascinating still were the reactions of other attendees, who were mostly German. The arena was packed on a midweek evening with nearly a thousand persons. A young German couple in their twenties noted that the exhibit was about to close and the show was quite popular. The bodies were not encased behind glass, merely located on stands or sometimes placed behind ropes. This did not prevent viewers from putting their faces only centimeters away from—or even slightly touching—the bodies. One of the more notable images was a figure that presumably held its own flayed skin, a rendition of a Renaissance anatomical drawing. At the end of the display was the ubiquitous museum shop selling items related to the exhibit. I found myself unable to resist buying a videotape, catalog, and T-shirt. Ironically, the videotape had footage from its first show in Japan, another country with a history of wartime medical experimentation on prisoners. In the past four years, the exhibit has traveled extensively in Europe, the United States and Asia. Despite the sensationalist and vexing ethical concerns that the exhibition raised, it explicitly emphasized the scientific contributions of and the need to learn from such bodies. Still, there remained lingering questions about the different kinds of life that bodies may have beyond death—a social life made possible with plastination—and about ways in which these bodies may come to represent the ideal body.

Chinese Bodies

I attended the "Universe Within" exhibit of plastinated bodies in Masonic Auditorium of San Francisco in spring 2005. The show followed on the heels of the Body Worlds 2 show held earlier in Los Angeles several months ago. At the S.F. exhibit, I met quite a few viewers who had attended the L.A. show several times. Alerted by my colleague, Carla Freccero, that the bodies were clearly Chinese, I went to study how this exhibit compared with the display in Berlin. The show was much smaller with fewer bodies, about fifty, and indeed the plastinated bodies, at least the whole ones, were clearly from non-European donors. Despite the lack of skin, the eyes and facial structure indicated their Chinese origin. A videotape of an interview with Dr. Sui Hongjin, confirmed that the bodies indeed originated from China and played continuously at two corners of the exhibit. Extensive attention has been paid to the origin of these bodies on the Chinese website devoted to plastinated bodies.

While race and the ethical procurement of these donor bodies were a critical part of this exhibit, gender was another focus of the display. Despite the removal of skin from some bodies, there was clear efforts to retain the genitalia. Moreover, in one case gender was elaborately tacked onto one figure. An aged female body had high heels and a handbag, ostensibly to illustrate the effects of such shoes on body posture. Near this body, in an unmarked case of body parts was the plastinated foot of a woman whose feet had been bound.

Similar to the exhibit in Berlin, the end of the show had a small museum shop as well as a comment book. I observed and spoke with participants who chose to enter their thoughts in this book. Many, like myself, also read through prior comments made by other viewers. Several genres were evident: praise, suggestions for improvement, dead-body jokes, and questions about the sources of these bodies. The question "Chinese prisons?" came up a dozen times in the volume that I read. In newspaper accounts about the S.F. show, two plastinated bodies were described as having what appeared to be bullet holes in the brain. Controversies have emerged at each venue where the plastinated bodies are exhibited. For instance, the S.F. show was marked by protests from Asian-American groups that claimed the bodies had transgressed "traditional" forms of funerary ritual and offended Buddhist beliefs. The L.A. show had a fetus stolen. In a sense, these events increased awareness of the exhibit and offered free publicity.

What follows is background about the origins of two different shows involving plastinated bodies—*BodyWorlds* and *The Universe Within*. Earlier in 2001, the journal *Nature* reported that Dr. Hagens had opened a plastination factory in Dalian, a port city on the Chinese eastern seaboard. This seemed to be a logical move, since the location offered cheap labor to process the plastinated bodies as well as ready access to corpses. Although Chinese state and medical authorities have been quick to disclaim any link to prisoner bodies, many donors may indeed come from morgues with unclaimed bodies and the sources for plastination are therefore not entirely clear.

The story of plastinated bodies and their display takes another twist in China. A display had dramatically opened in Beijing earlier in 2004 with mainly Chinese bodies from the Dalian factory. The proliferation of plastinated bodies from

China have produced competing shows with the BodyWorlds exhibits, which are officially sanctioned and associated with Dr. Hagens. Once the technique was introduced in Dalian, the lack of trademark protections meant that the techniques could be shared and spread widely across the country's medical schools. Cheap labor will not only produce inexpensive sneakers or toys but also literally cheap bodies.

The circulation of plastinated bodies at times parallel the organ trade, which has established official routes as well as illicit conduits that often intertwine (Scheper-Hughes 2004). In Europe and the United States, elaborate information about the ethical donation process is always provided (Sharp 2005). Similarly, the Chinese medical schools that have undertaken plastination emphasize their ethical procurement of bodies. Such attention to ethical issues indirectly underscores uneasy concerns about whether a donor has truly been a donor. The display of plastinated bodies, whether whole or in parts, raises key questions about aspects of the human condition that dead bodies represent and about the violence that is undertaken to produce them. Unlike organs that are procured mainly from bodies that have been subject to violent accidents, plastination can be applied to bodies in all conditions.

In seeing and thinking about these dead bodies, I find myself asking why I still feel unsettled about their exhibition, a response that many attendees have reported to me. Is it because these dead bodies may once have been animated, were embodied selves, felt the sensations of a delicious meal and the tactility of warm ocean waves? Is it because we think dead bodies are meant to go away and disappear, to be placed in the ground. scattered in ashes, or offered up in a Tibetan sky burial? Is this the other inside? Or closer to home, why does the morbid anthropologist in me insist on witnessing the spectacle and transformation of dead bodies in displays about the human condition?

Plastinated bodies simultaneously confront the senses with corpses while desensitizing viewers to the violence involved in producing them.

Sharon Kaufman's suggestion in this volume that we are all potential donors or recipients emphasizes the ability of medicine and technology to extend life through organ transplants and other interventions. These technologies often illuminate illogics of the political economy, which allows 90% of our health care costs to be incurred in the last years of our lives. For you see, death marks the ultimate failure of medicine. Yet, the inevitable sense that we will all become dead bodies one day is disrupted by the possibility that a cadaveric body may actually live on and become a different subject.

This is a story with a transformative ending. A post-human body in the making. Perhaps that is the vexing allure and promise that plastination offers. Rather than relying on cryogenics and revival through future technology, plastination suggests tangible and visible forms of bodily transformation beyond death in the present.

Bibliography

Cartwright, Lisa, *Screening the Body: Tracing Medicine's Visual Culture.* Minneapolis: University of Minnesota Press, 1995.

Scheper-Hughes, Nancy, "Parts Unknown: Undercover Ethnography of the Organs—Trafficking Underworld" in *Ethnography* 5(1): 29–73. 2004.

———"The Global Traffic in Organs." *Current Anthropology* 41 (2):191–224. 2000.

Scheper-Hughes, Nancy and Philippe Bourgois, eds. *Violence in War and Peace: An Anthology.* London: Basil Blackwell, 2003.

Sharp, Lesley. *Bodies, Commodities, and Biotechnologies.* The 2004 Leonard Hastings Schoff Memorial Lectures, Columbia University. New York: Columbia University Press, 2006.

Treichler, Paula A., Lisa Cartwright, and Constance Penley, eds. *The Visible Woman: Imaging Technologies, Gender, and Science.* New York: New York University Press, 1998.

Contributors

Virginia L. Blum is Professor of English and Director of the Committee on Social Theory at the University of Kentucky.

Aleshia Brevard is a writer who lives and works in the Santa Cruz mountains. The author of *The Woman I Was Not to Be* (Temple University Press 2001), she taught stagecraft and directed main stage productions at East Tennessee State University after many years as an actor in film, television, and theater.

Joyce Brodsky is Professor Emerita from the art departments of the University of Connecticut, Storrs and the University of California Santa Cruz. Her forthcoming book *Experiences of Passage: The Paintings of Yun Gee and Li-lan*, deals with cosmopolitanism and transnationalism.

Nancy N. Chen is associate professor in Anthropology at the University of California Santa Cruz. She is author of *Breathing Spaces: Qigong, Psychiatry, and Healing in China* (Columbia 2003).

Maria Frangos is a graduate student in literature at the University of California Santa Cruz. She is completing a dissertation on monstrous female bodies: "Mélusine and Her 'Daughters': A Genealogy of Female Monstrosity and Metamorphosis from the Middle Ages through Early Modernity."

Carla Freccero is professor of literature, feminist studies, and history of consciousness at UCSC. A specialist in early modern cultural studies, US popular culture, and feminist and queer theory, her most recent book is *Queer/Early/Modern* (Duke UP 2005).

Joanna Frueh is a writer and artist best known for her performance art and writing on the erotic, beauty, gender, and art. Her latest book is *Swooning Beauty: A Memoir of Pleasure* (2006).

Shelby Graham is director and curator of the Mary Porter Sesnon Art Gallery at the University of California Santa Cruz. She holds a MFA in photography and teaches classes in museum and gallery practices. Her most recent curatorial work is the exhibition *Image as Object* (2006).

Donna Haraway is a professor in the History of Consciousness Department at the University of California Santa Cruz, where she teaches feminist theory, science studies, and animal studies. She is at work on a book, *When Species Meet*.

Sharon R. Kaufman is professor of medical anthropology at the University of California, San Francisco. Her recent research explores life extension, technologies of dying, and subjectification in an aging society. She is the author, most recently, of *And a Time to Die: How American Hospitals Shape the End of Life* (Scribner, 2005).

Steve Kurzman is an anthropologist and has studied prosthetics in the United States, India, and Cambodia. He lives in the San Francisco Bay Area, where he works as a research consultant.

John Marlovits is a PhD candidate and Teaching Fellow in the Department of Anthropology at the University of California Santa Cruz. His dissertation explores the cultural and historical aspects of mental illness. He has conducted ethnographic field research in community mental health centers and with advocacy groups in Seattle, Washington.

Helene Moglen holds the Presidential Chair in Literature at the University of California Santa Cruz, where she is also the Director of the Institute for Advanced Feminist Research. She has published in the areas of literary criticism, feminist theory and education. Her most recent book is *The Trauma of Gender: A Feminist Theory of the English Novel* (University of California Press, 2001.)

Megan Moodie is a Teaching Fellow and PhD candidate in anthropology at the University of California Santa Cruz. Her work is concerned with questions of gendered citizenship in the north Indian state of Rajasthan and in the US military.

Sheila Namir is a training and supervising analyst at the Institute of Contemporary Psychoanalysis in Los Angeles and a clinical psychologist and psychoanalyst practicing in Santa Cruz. She was on the faculties of UCLA Medical School, California

School of Professional Psychology and the Southern California Psychoanalytic Institute in Los Angeles for more than twenty years. She has published in the areas of psychosocial aspects of AIDS and cancer, medical psychology, trauma and feminist psychoanalysis.

Victoria Pitts is Associate Professor of Sociology at Queens College and the Graduate Center, City University of New York. She is the author of *In the Flesh: The Cultural Politics of Body Modification* (Palgrave/MacMillan, 2003). Her forthcoming book is entitled *Surgery Junkies: The Cultural Boundaries of Cosmetic Surgery*.

Lorna A. Rhodes teaches medical anthropology, the anthropology of institutions, and ethnographic research methods at the University of Washington. She is the author of *Emptying Beds: The Work of an Emergency Psychiatric Unit* (University of California Press, 1991) and *Total Confinement: Madness and Reason in the Maximum Security Prison* (University of California Press, 2004).

Kelley Richardson is an award-winning artist and photographer. A graduate of the San Francisco Art Institute, she completed her fine arts degree in photography. Her forthcoming book is based on three years of exploring and documenting tattoo culture in Santa Cruz, California through the lens of her camera.

Ann J. Russ is a medical anthropologist and member of the research faculty at the University of California, San Francisco.

Gabriela Sandoval is Assistant Professor of Sociology at the University of California Santa Cruz. Her research focuses on Latino/a sociology, voting and representational politics, urban sociology, and political sociology.

Janet K. Shim is assistant adjunct professor in the Department of Social and Behavioral Sciences at the University of California, San Francisco.

Mary Weaver is a graduate student in the History of Consciousness department at UCSC. Her dissertation will address questions of transgender and transsexual embodiment, epistemology and ontology.